# KISS YOUR
# BUT
## *GOOD-BYE*

## HOW TO GET BEYOND
## THE ONE WORD THAT STANDS
## BETWEEN YOU & SUCCESS

## JOSEPH AZELBY & ROBERT AZELBY

HarperCollins books may be purchased for educational, business, or sales promotional use. For information, please e-mail the Special Markets Department at SPsales@harpercollins.com.

FIRST EDITION

*Designed by Renato Stanisic*

Library of Congress Cataloging-in-Publication Data
    Azelby, Joseph.
      Kiss your but good-bye : how to get beyond the one word that stands between you and success / Joseph Azelby and Robert Azelby.—First edition.
         pages cm
      ISBN 978-0-06-224698-1 (Hardcover)
      ISBN 978-0-06-228785-4 (International Edition)
      1. Career development. 2. Performance. 3. Self-actualization (Psychology)
    4. Success in business. I. Azelby, Robert. II. Title.
    HF5381.A94    2013
    650.1—dc23

                                                     2013003925

13  14  15  16  17   OV/RRD   10  9  8  7  6  5  4  3  2  1

To our mother, Theresa Marie Azelby,
the best mom that ever lived.

# ACKNOWLEDGMENTS

We want to thank everyone who made this book possible. Our wives, Janet and Michele, who allowed us to write undisturbed as the normal chaos of family life ensued. Our combined eight children, Christine, Colleen, and Jackie on the east coast and Katie, Anna, Joe, Sammy, and Robbie on the west coast, who watched two grown men write, edit, argue, and laugh over the phone as this book took shape. The older children were coerced to read what we thought were particularly clever paragraphs. They would pat us on the shoulder and politely say, "Yeah, that's great, Dad," and flee. A big thank-you goes to our eighty-six-year-old dad, Joe Azelby Sr., who passed along his storytelling prowess to all of his offspring; Terri, our sister, who dove deep into the documents and made edits and suggestions that brought coherency to the text; our brother, Tom, whose humor, antics, and boxing skills made this book far more interesting; and all of our friends who read the book and provided suggestions and comments.

Special thanks to John Rice, who provided English grammar, punctuation, and wit to the document, and to Bill Davis, who pushed us to write the book. Thanks to Dan, our cousin, who claims he read a couple of the draft chapters, but we'll never really know because he gave us no feedback. (We promised that his pathetic effort would be acknowledged.) Thanks, Jeffrey Krames, our agent and editor, who deeply believed in the project and claims it saved his life. In convincing us to retain him as editor and agent, Jeffrey said he would take his own life if forced to work on another traditional leadership or management book. Jeffrey's immense literary talents and maniacal work ethic brought order, rhythm, and more humor to the project. Thanks to our publisher, Hollis Heimbouch, and the HarperCollins team, who immediately understood how this book could help the people who read it. The Harper folks have been fantastic partners in every respect. The creation of the book has been a gift to the two guys who wrote it. We hope you have as much fun reading it.

# CONTENTS

# PREFACE

We grew up in Dumont, New Jersey, a small suburban town located fifteen miles from midtown Manhattan. Our dad was a New York City police officer, so "the City" and all of its problems and politics were part of our childhood experience. For that reason we have always dreamed of owning a family farm that all of our siblings and their children could enjoy. Perhaps we long for a simpler life or a place far away from the crowded cities and suburban sprawl. When we were both living on the east coast we would go farm shopping. Every so often a farm for sale, advertised in the newspaper or on the Internet, would pique our interest. On a Sunday, we would grab a couple of the kids and take a ride to rural western New Jersey, the Lehigh Valley of Pennsylvania, or upstate New York to check it out.

On one particular excursion, a farmer selling his sixty-acre farm took us to see the beautiful pond that he had built a few years back. He told us that the pond was filled with large-mouth bass, crappies, and some perch.

We asked, "So you stocked it?"

He said, "No, I didn't do anything." We could not see any other ponds or streams in the area, so we were curious.

We then asked, "If you didn't stock the pond, how did the fish get there?"

He said, "I just built the pond and the fish showed up."

We were now standing there wondering if this farmer was just messing with us or having fun with the kids. We said something to the effect of "Fish can't live long out of water, and we've never seen a fish walk. How did these fish get in a new pond if you didn't put them there?"

"That's easy," he said. "The ducks brought them." He went on to explain that when ducks land in a fish pond, they stir up the fish eggs. The eggs then stick to the ducks' down feathers. When the ducks fly and land in another pond, the fish eggs are released into that new location. That's how fish get to a new pond.

That day that farmer taught our children and us something that we have never forgotten. We believe that you, too, will learn something from this book that you will never forget. Our hope is that, like new life coming to new waters, the messages of *Kiss Your BUT Good-Bye* will travel from one pond to another, bringing to you a sense of self-awareness that will renew your career and make the lives of everyone with whom you interact a little more enjoyable.

# INTRODUCTION

This book is not for CEOs seeking transformational leadership. It's not for global business titans who want to teach their elephant-sized companies how to dance. This book will not show you how to take a company from good to great. This book is about something more important . . . you. Where do you want to take your career, and what's preventing you from doing so? The following pages will force you to take a very hard look at your job, your performance in that job, and why you may not be advancing as quickly as you hoped or expected. This book will not teach you how to play to your strengths. You should do that naturally. Rather, this book was written to help you identify your weaknesses. In the business world, the people who can leverage their strengths and manage their weaknesses most often achieve their career aspirations. We are going to take you where you don't want to go but where you really need to go.

If you want to get better at what you do, keep reading. If

you want to expose and correct your weaknesses and obtain a better understanding of the behaviors that are undermining your progression, keep reading. If you want to improve your management effectiveness and improve how you support your manager, keep reading. If you want to overhaul how you are perceived by others, keep reading. If you are prepared to take full responsibility for your situation, keep reading. If you refuse to be a victim, keep reading. If you want the truth, keep reading.

Now, let's go on a journey that will help you see yourself the way others see you. By doing so, you can find and break down the barriers you have built between yourself and the personal success that you deserve.

We have worked for Fortune 500 companies for a combined forty years. Younger brother Bob is with a large California biopharmaceutical firm, and older brother Joe works in New York at a large financial institution. Over the last two decades we have had many discussions about how employees' behaviors and managerial perceptions create career "enhancers" and "derailers" that impact and determine career progression. We have observed how some careers advance due to certain behaviors and perceptions, while others stall or falter. We call each other often for advice and perspective when we have to deal with the thorniest business management issues. Those issues almost always involve people and the things they do or don't do that make work harder and less pleasant than it should be. While it's easy to point out the flaws in others, the "they" can just as easily turn to "I," because it is often one of us causing unnecessary problems. The many issues and situations that we have experienced and discussed could fill a book. So we decided to take the things we have learned and write them down so that you can learn from the things we have witnessed or done that undermine careers and teams.

Reading this book will be a very good use of your time. You'll receive forty years of human observation, employee analysis, and solution-oriented advice in the brief time it will take you to get through it. We both have a touch of business-induced ADD, and we assume you do, too. The book is a quick read, and we did our best to make it light, casual, and interesting. We provide examples, make our points, and move on. Thankfully, we did not write this book to make money. Very few people can make a living writing, and we are extremely confident that we can't, either. We wrote this book to share our experiences and insights. We believe it will help others free themselves from the attitudes and behaviors that are impeding their career progress and straining their relationships at work and at home.

This book is titled *Kiss Your BUT Good-Bye*. Don't worry; it's not an exercise book, and it is not about the next fad diet. (You can deal with that problem on your own by eating Subway sandwiches or going on *The Biggest Loser*.) This book will not help you quit smoking—but common sense and a will to live should. The "but" we want to help you to "kiss good-bye" is the BUT that is holding you back in your career. This BUT we speak of is shaping how everyone at your company thinks of you; senior executives, your direct manager, your peers, and your direct reports see you through a prism that your BUT has created. If together we can kick this BUT, or at least shrink it, we'll improve how you are perceived at work and change your career trajectory for the better.

We are confident that if we can get you focused on your BUT, you can get a bigger and better job than the one you have today. In this book, we'll tell you the things you need to do more of and the things you need to do less of. We'll tell you things you should do all of the time and some things that you should never, ever do. A loftier title, a higher salary, and a lot more job satisfaction are what you will gain if you take what we have written to heart.

Let's get back to this BUT thing. Everybody has a BUT. We will review many BUTs in the upcoming chapters. Some will be yours, and you must recognize them, accept them, and manage them aggressively. Other BUTs will belong to your colleagues, and you must help them do the same. If you live a full life or work in a business setting long enough, you will have direct experience with all of these BUTs. As you progress in your career, it becomes increasingly important that you become adept at recognizing BUTs and coaching your people on how to manage them. As a leader, if you don't manage the BUTs of your direct reports, there is no doubt you'll start to grow a BUT of your own. Remember, everybody has a BUT, but we want yours to be smaller than everyone else's in your company. Now we will show you why.

Imagine a workplace where every person is aware of the things they do or fail to do that are preventing them from being more productive and valuable employees. Imagine a company where everyone speaks openly and honestly about their weaknesses and is committed to improving them. Imagine an environment where colleagues help each other become more efficient and less disruptive by always speaking the truth. Imagine a place where the firm's most talented employees know exactly what they need to do to attain a leadership position.

That place can exist. This book can help create it. Read it, and pass it along to a colleague, and require that he or she do the same. In the near future, we can all work in that place.

# CHAPTER 1

# THE BUT

Next time you are part of a formal or informal business discussion that involves an employee's work performance or personal qualities, we want you to listen closely for the most important word to be spoken. That word is "but." It usually comes in the middle of a statement, most often right after a compliment. As soon as "but" is uttered, people lean forward in their chairs in anxious anticipation to hear what imperfection or affliction one of their colleagues may have.

This is what we're talking about:

"Jim is a great marketer, *but* he can't close the deals."

"Rachel works hard, *but* she can't prioritize."

"Larry is a great producer, *but* he's a lousy manager."

"Steven is an effective individual performer, *but* he doesn't leverage the network."

"Samantha is good at tasks, *but* she is not a strategic thinker."

"Lisa has plenty of IQ, *but* she has no EQ whatsoever."

Right now you are saying, "Oh, I get it. 'But,' that's a really clever word, and you're right. People say that all the time when they talk about other people at work." There's more to this little word, however, than meets the eye.

We don't know what your BUT looks like, and we certainly don't know how big it is. We also don't know what your colleagues' BUTs look like or how big they are. We do know, however, that you and your teammates have BUTs, because everyone we have ever met has at least one. Our mission is to help you find your BUT. We will make you stare at your BUT and show you the BUTs of your coworkers. We'll discuss your BUT and help you get your hands firmly around it so that you can control it. Then we are going to give you some proven tools and methods to shrink your BUT so that you have the smallest one among all of your peers.

We have heard countless excuses and whining from people who are not progressing in their careers. It's amazing how many people blame others for their situation, or how many make up reasons or excuses for why they are unfulfilled or underutilized in their current job. Some of our favorite pathetic excuses: "I don't manage up well," "I refuse to kiss ass," "Promotions are political," or "Only diversity candidates were considered for that assignment." These ideas allow people to feel better about themselves. They are, however, merely excuses for failure that mask the truth.

Let's start with a very common BUT that is well known in almost every office. We're sure you can name a few colleagues with this particular affliction.

---

## BUT BREAK: THE TALKER
### "Cassandra is really smart, *but* she never shuts up."

"You Talk Too Much" was a 1961 hit record by Joe Jones. You don't want your manager singing this song about you. People who talk too much make their managers worry they will screw up a client presentation or suck the energy out of the next management committee meeting. If you speak a lot more than you listen, you most likely have a problem. In fact, you may even have a nickname like "Chatty Kathy" or "Mr. Blah Blah Blah."

Every company has someone who has perfected the art of talking long after everyone else has stopped listening. This BUT is particularly annoying if the person talks mostly about himself or herself. Once the Talker gets on a roll, they are like the bus in the movie *Speed*. No matter how many times you try to knock their chatter off the road, somehow it just keeps going. How is it that they talk so much and say so little? And when they do it with clients, you have to muster every ounce of composure to stop yourself from strangling them.

If you are an incessant talker, please stop now! It's killing your ability to advance. Self-awareness is one of the most important qualities of a leader, and talking too much is the surest sign you lack that important quality. You may not be the number-one "motor mouth" in your office, but if you are ranked in the top 10 percent, we guarantee it's holding you back. In the history of mankind, no one has ever learned anything while they were talking. If you are presenting, take a breath every so often, look around, and see if your audience is with you or simply sleeping with their eyes open. Early in Joe's career an old banker colleague pulled him aside after a meeting in which he had gone on for too long on a topic. He said, "Joe, you just blew a perfect opportunity to keep your mouth shut." His comment had such an impact that Joe still remembers it twenty-three years later.

**SOLUTION:** If you suspect that talking too much is your BUT, we suggest that the next time you have an important meeting where you will be speaking, take one of those large black steel binder clips that hold big stacks of paper together and clip it to the end of your tongue. Leave it on for one minute just before the meeting starts. This will remind you just how much your tongue is hurting you.

In all seriousness, when speaking to your audience make sure you pay attention to the body language of the attendees. Are they looking back at you or staring into space? Do they seem interested or engaged? Are they asking questions, or are they checking their smartphones or doodling on their notepads? If you feel you have lost the audience, you have to try to get them back. Ask them if this is the information they wanted. Ask them if you should move on to the next section. Ask them what they would like to discuss. Make them engage with you. The best presentations are those that are interactive between speaker and audience. When presenting, you are, in essence, delivering a product to your important customer base. Give them exactly what they want, with no filler, and elicit the feedback you need to make sure that you can keep doing so.

---

In our experience, the major reason people's careers do not advance is they are either lacking a skill, which disqualifies them for advancement, or they have a behavior that is annoying or destructive. The reason the promotion or best project goes to that other person is the hiring manager believes the other person is better than you. People will go to great lengths to convince themselves otherwise, but their BUT is what's really standing in the way of their advancement.

Remember, every company is competing against other companies in their industry, and they want to win. Companies know that people make all the difference, and they want the most talented people in the biggest roles. Don't get caught up in the blame game. Take ownership of your career, and remember your situation is a result of the actions and behaviors you control—your BUTs. In the corporate world, it's the people with the smallest BUTs that rise the fastest and go the furthest. BUTs are like bad habits. They have to be acknowledged, accepted, and aggressively managed.

## YOU HAVE A BUT

Let's suppose you graduated summa cum laude from Duke University, and you received your MBA from Penn's Wharton School. You are on the fast track for promotion at your market-leading firm. You are bright, attractive, ambitious, aggressive, and confident. You have impeccable taste in all wardrobe matters. When you look at your face in the mirror every morning you see perfection, endless possibility, and a future CEO.

Unfortunately, your manager and your colleagues don't look into your magic mirror, and they definitely don't see Prince Charming or Snow White. The thing they're most focused on is your BUT. As we pointed out earlier, we guarantee you have one. Perhaps you have more than one. It's hard to see your BUT in a mirror. In fact, you really need to hold up a second mirror to see it. Think of this book as your rearview mirror, because it will show you things only others can see.

We are going to describe for you a variety of BUTs. Some you will instantly recognize as those of your colleagues. More important, you need to recognize your own BUTs. This book was written for you.

Everyone is naturally the center of his or her own universe. However, if you spend so much time focusing inward instead of on everything that is orbiting around you, then you will inevitably miss things, good and bad, that will impact your career. A big step to confronting your BUT is to know just how small your own personal star system is in the grand scope of the corporate universe.

---

## BUT BREAK: REPLACEABLE
**"Jay exudes confidence, *but* he believes he is irreplaceable."**

The Bible says that "pride cometh before the fall." The moment you start believing that you can't be replaced is the beginning of the end. It's much like the overconfident sports team on the cover of *Sports Illustrated* that believes it can't be beaten. They stop working hard, and they lose their edge when they no longer respect opponents. They fail to do the little things that make the big difference, because they don't feel they need to. That's when they start losing. We are all replaceable, and we should never forget it. There is a talented colleague in your office who would love to have your job. And there is an army of talent in the market looking for good jobs like yours. If you act like you are irreplaceable, you may come to the office one day and find all of your personal effects packed up.

Last spring Joe's daughter, Colleen, was studying in Spain. Joe had business to do in Paris, so he had her meet him there for the weekend. They took the opportunity to visit the catacombs, a series of caverns and tunnels under Paris that hold the remains of more than six million Parisians. The skulls and bones of all these people are stacked from floor to ceiling in a never-ending trail of underground rooms. It is a macabre yet humbling experience of the first order. We're sure most of the six million people whose bones are stacked up like firewood in the catacombs, at some time in their life, felt irreplaceable.

**SOLUTION:** Never let up. Compete every day. Be paranoid about the competition. The more knowledgeable and productive you are, the more difficult you are to replace.

# PEOPLE ARE TALKING ABOUT YOUR BUT

We can almost guarantee you that in the hallways and conference rooms of your office, your BUT is being discussed. Your BUT is a multimedia sensation! It is being talked about over the phone, discussed via email, texted across state lines, and is the catalyst for giggles around the water cooler. Your BUT may have been recently featured in a talent-review PowerPoint presentation with your name and face right next to it. Your colleagues and your manager tell stories and jokes about it that make them laugh—or make them furious. People just love talking about your BUT, especially your peers, who take every opportunity to bring it up. They look much better if they keep everyone focused on your BUT rather than their own.

If you spend a lot of time talking about other people's BUTs, then you may very well have a BUT of your own. Even though you might be in possession of some juicy info that will make you popular at the water cooler, the more you gossip, the less your coworkers will trust you.

---

## BUT BREAK: CONFIDENTIALITY

**"Randy means well, *but* he loves to gossip."**

In every organization, there is an inner circle of key people. This group would of course include senior management but may also include people not that high on the org chart. Let's call this group the circle of trust. If you want to stay in the circle of trust in your company, you must be able to keep confidential information . . . well, you know, just that: confidential. Don't tell colleagues other people's secrets. If subordinates, peers, or managers share things with you in confidence, keep them to yourself. We know information is power, and you can't wait to show off what you know, but you need to fight the urge and keep it to yourself. Joe once had a colleague who said, "It's not that I can't keep a secret. It's just that everyone I tell can't keep a secret." It's that type of logic that will get you thrown out of the circle of trust.

**SOLUTION:** In the navy there is an expression, "Loose lips sink ships." In the business world: "Loose lips torpedo careers." Avoid the water-cooler chatter. Keep confidential what has been classified as confidential. Don't blow a perfect opportunity to keep your mouth shut.

---

Guess who your colleagues aren't talking to about your BUT? You! And you need to know this. Your colleagues are having too much fun with your BUT to tell you about it. They will spend hours—days, even weeks—discussing it with each other, but never with you. They know if they disclose it to you, you may stop exposing it. This will ruin all the fun and open up the possibility of their BUT shining in the spotlight. They want your BUT to hold you back so they can advance instead. A competitive peer telling you about your BUT would be like Patriots quarterback Tom Brady waving and pointing to Jets cornerback Darelle Revis to let him know he is out of position. This just does not happen in the full-contact competition of professional football or office politics.

Some BUTs are funny, but others just bring aggravation. Here's a BUT that is sure to be grumbled about behind your back.

---

## BUT BREAK: HIGH MAINTENANCE
### "Jack is smart and ambitious, *but* he's really high maintenance."

There are people who, while doing their job, needlessly burn the time and energy of everyone around them. They create an incessant array of meetings, phone calls, emails, and conflict-resolution sessions that inundate their manager and colleagues. High-maintenance people need more help, more encouragement, and more handholding than their colleagues. They are often more emotional and easily slighted. These personal qualities create time-wasting activities for everyone around them.

Such distractions sharply raise the cost of employing this individual and greatly reduce their value to their firm. For example, a high-maintenance employee may be paid $75,000 per year, but their cost to the firm can be $150,000 if you account for the resources they drain from the company.

The problem with high-maintenance people is they are often oblivious to the immeasurable cost of their never-ending needs and attention grabbing. They can be hardworking, friendly, and very well intentioned. However, they involve others with their problems and challenges way too early and way too often. High-maintenance people are very squeaky and require a lot of oil. And oil is very expensive. This BUT affects so many people and it's definitely one that will get you noticed—in a bad way.

**SOLUTION:** First, assess whether you could be perceived as high maintenance. How much of your manager's and colleagues' time is being taken up by issues that you have responsibility for? Remember, you are getting paid to manage these issues, and your job is to protect others from having to deal with them. If you are high maintenance, you'd better deliver some high productivity. Otherwise, your antics will not be tolerated for very long. Think carefully before bringing your problems to others and burning up their time. Try to solve things on your own. Your manager has plenty of other things to do. If you do show up at your manager's door with a problem, make sure that you also bring a solution. Companies are looking for people who deliver high productivity and require a low level of maintenance. The deadly combination of high maintenance and low productivity will kill any career.

---

Your coworkers base their opinion about you mainly around your BUT. Even if you don't feel like your BUT is as big as it is—if you know about it at all—your estimation of yourself is not reality. Your reality is based on everyone else's opinion about you.

## PERCEPTION IS REALITY

We've said it before. We'll say it again. Everyone has a BUT.

Yes, even we, your beloved authors, have BUTs of our own. Bob used to have a really big BUT. It wasn't until his manager delivered the truth that he realized how colleagues' perception of him mattered most.

Bob was a successful regional sales director running a team with outstanding sales numbers. He spent a lot of time in the field with his salespeople removing obstacles and getting them the resources and support they needed. He was looking forward to his annual review with the national sales director, and his expectations on his performance rating were very high.

The meeting with his boss started like this: "Bob, we have a problem. It's actually *your* problem, but I'm the only one dealing with it right now." Bob was stunned and confused. His manager went on: "The people in the home office say you are a bully. Not only do you bulldoze right over them, but you never even look down at their crushed bodies to say thank you."

Bob pushed back on his manager and said, "That's not true. The people in the home office like me, and I do appreciate what they do."

The sales director said, "Bob, it does not matter what *you* think! What matters is how they feel and what they think about you. If they think you are a bully, then you are."

Bob's manager exposed his BUT to extreme sunlight, and Bob got burned. Yet when he got over the shock and denial, Bob knew his boss was right and that damage control was in order. Bob was so focused on the sales numbers that he had been a jerk to the people who were helping deliver them. Needless to say, Bob was landing hard on his coworkers, and they didn't like it. Bob's boss didn't like it either. Former General Electric CEO Jack Welch cared about the company's numbers, but he would not tolerate even the greatest producer if he was a jerk who bullied his people. To fix his BUT, Bob immediately went into relationship-repair mode. He started thanking people in the home office for everything they did. He sent handwritten thank-you notes and mailed hundred-dollar gift cards to people who went beyond the call of duty for his team. From that day forward, Bob made sure that his colleagues in the home office and his manager felt appreciated for all they had done for him.

Bob's boss was spot-on when he said it only matters what they think. We all like to think we control our own destiny and that we manage our own careers. Unfortunately, we are only partially correct. With very few exceptions, our destiny, our careers, and our livelihood depend on how others perceive us. If your manager perceives you as lazy, do you expect you will be given more responsibility? If your peers perceive you as selfish, will they want to partner with you on an important project? If your subordinates don't like or trust you, do you think they will go beyond the call of duty to correct one of your mistakes?

In order to advance and be successful in business, you must be perceived by the people around you as someone who deserves to be successful. Business is a team game, and it's the people around you who provide you the opportunity to be successful. The people above you must be willing to pull you up to the next level. The people below you must carry you on their shoulders and lift you up. Meanwhile, the peers around you must support you enough so as not to undermine or sabotage your ascension. Green Bay Packers quarterback Aaron Rodgers can't complete passes without a strong offensive line obsessed with protecting him. Jimmie Johnson can't win NASCAR races without a passionate and expert pit crew prepared for almost any scenario. Aaron's offensive line and Jimmie's pit crew believe their guy deserves to win, and that's why they work for them. The world of business is no different. You must be perceived by your colleagues as someone who deserves to win, or we can assure you that you won't.

Here is the key point: People's perception of you is your reality whether you like it or not. And they will make you or break you.

You likely aren't aware of the power of your attitude in the workplace, but your coworkers don't have a choice but to deal with your demeanor. Positive energy is the fuel that inspires individuals to do their very best work and drives their team to excel. Negative energy, which is the by-product of complaining, is the corporate equivalent of slashing tires. You might feel like you gain camaraderie with your colleagues by pointing out the negatives, but in the reality of their perception, you are likely alienating everyone around you.

---

## BUT BREAK: BITCH AND MOAN

**"Steven is smooth and articulate with clients,
*but* he complains about everything."**

There are some people in an organization who just suck the energy out of a team because all they do is complain. "We don't have enough resources." "Why do we have to fly coach versus business class?" "I got screwed on my bonus." "My boss is an idiot." "My assistant is brain-dead . . . blah blah blah." It never ends. The worst thing about these complainers is when they are in front of their manager or other senior executives they often say everything is going great, and they wave the corporate flag. These people believe they are smooth operators and they know how to work the system. The truth of the matter is everybody in the organization knows they are unappreciative, self-centered jerks . . . even their bosses.

**SOLUTION:** If you are an endless complainer, you need to change immediately. Listen to yourself. Why are you so miserable? Stop complaining and start fixing the things that bother you so much about the company. That's what responsibility and leadership are all about, and that's what you are getting paid for.

If you can't fix things, then do everyone a favor—including yourself—and go work somewhere else. Please leave now! Go find a place where you will be happy. It will save your manager the time and aggravation it takes to surgically remove the cancerous tumor you have become. Your manager cannot allow your bad attitude to metastasize and contaminate the entire firm. You will be amputated if you don't knock it off.

If you work with a complainer, explain to them how their bad attitude is negatively impacting you and your colleagues.

If they simply don't care, suggest they go work somewhere that does not make them so miserable. Hopefully they will listen and self-select out. If not, take immediate action or advise those who can. As you can see, we don't have a lot of patience for this insidious BUT.

---

On the flip side of negativity is a degree of positivity that merely highlights how out of touch you are with reality. The solution to being too negative is not being the polar opposite. If you come to every situation, both good and bad, with a big smile on your face, you will soon lose your credibility.

---

## BUT BREAK: MR. BRIGHTSIDE
**"I like that Charles is upbeat and positive,
*but* at times he borders on delusional."**

"Mr. Brightside" is a song by the Killers that topped the charts in 2004. The song describes a young man's anguish that a woman he loves is being seduced by another man. Ironically, in the midst of all this agony is the curious lyrical refrain of "I'm Mr. Brightside." If you are Mr. Brightside in the office, you have some work to do.

While optimism can be a wonderful personal characteristic, your positive attitude needs to be grounded in reality. A business will not improve or become more competitive just by someone wishing or saying it will. Hoping for a better future does little to secure a better future. If you are always optimistic without a strategy or actions to justify your optimism, you will lose credibility with your colleagues and managers.

**SOLUTION:** Be realistic at all times. Here is a great adage we always refer to: "If you are able to keep a cool head while everyone around you is panicking, you probably don't understand the severity of the situation." If you have problems, talk about them and deal with them—don't just glaze over them. If you see opportunities, lay out the specific steps that need to be taken to capture them. Provide specific facts and measurable trends that underpin the reasons for your optimism. Show people that you have a balanced view of the risks and rewards your business faces and manages every day.

---

The entire concept of "perception is reality" is that every day the people around you are evaluating both your character and your competence. They have to perceive you as being of very high quality in order for you to advance. It really matters how you are perceived by those around you, because they help create your reality.

**Wrap-up:** We would not be surprised if you are still skeptical about the existence or size of your own BUT. You might even be optimistic about some of the little phrases we've offered, like "Cassandra is really smart, *but* she never shuts up." At least everyone is saying Cassandra is really smart, right?

Wrong. Once you say the word "but," the listener forgets all of the positive statements spoken prior. Your BUT is the great nullifier of anything good about you.

We bet you know people who talk too much, complain constantly, or are overly positive. Perhaps the names and faces of family members, in-laws, colleagues, or bosses popped into your mind when we reviewed these BUTs. You can't help but associate these common BUTs with people you know. And guess what. These BUTs shape your opinion of them. In turn your BUTs are shaping others' opinion of you. You are doing or saying things that are creating a negative workplace profile. You are not doing or saying other things, which is why others are rated higher than you at review time. If you have not yet found your BUT, read on, more are coming. Now lock your ego in a closet. Drop your defenses. Engage your self-awareness. Open your mind to the possibility that you are less than perfect. The truth hurts, and the truth will set you free. Let's go find it together.

# CHAPTER 2

# FINDING YOUR BUT

We hope by now you have accepted the fact that you have a BUT. Now you must become a Truth Seeker and begin your mission to find it. It's out there, and everyone else can see it. You must pursue it. You must arrest it. You must prosecute it. Then you can conquer it.

## PUTTING OUT AN APB ON YOUR BUT

Anybody familiar with crime dramas, from *Dragnet* to *NYPD Blue*, knows that when cops put out an APB, they're looking for an armed and dangerous criminal. Well, your BUT is armed and dangerous, so you'd better put out an APB if you want it locked up. But in the case of BUTs, APB doesn't mean "All Points Bulletin." Instead, it stands for Aptitude, Personality, and Behavior.

- A is for Aptitude: An innate component of a competency to do a certain kind of work at a certain level
  *Translation*: Are you good at something or not?
- P is for Personality: The pattern of feelings, thoughts, and activities that distinguishes one person from another
  *Translation*: This is just who you are. It's coded in your DNA.
- B is for Behavior: The manner in which one conducts oneself when acting or responding to external stimuli
  *Translation*: How do you act when you are working alone or working with others in various situations?

The APB describes both the root causes and the symptoms of each and every BUT out there. People develop BUTs when they lack the aptitude for certain tasks their job requires. Many BUTs are a true reflection of personality. Other BUTs come about because of people's behaviors that may annoy their colleagues or undermine their performance.

BUTs can be caused by any of these three factors, and in most cases, one factor often contributes to the other. If you are naturally impatient (personality), you might prematurely take action (behavior) before you have completed the due diligence warranted prior to committing to a project. A person who is shy and timid (personality) is not going to be good at cold-calling (aptitude) and may show up late for work every day (behavior), because they hate their job. Additionally, not attending the sales training course (behavior) because you think you don't need to (personality) can weaken your sales skills (aptitude) relative to those of your peers.

Here's the APB at work:

## BUT BREAK: JEKYLL AND HYDE
**"Ben is very capable, *but* he's so moody."**

Nobody wants to work with a moody person. You never know who is going to show up to work—will it be Dr. Jekyll or Mr. Hyde? Moody people can set a bad tone for the day as soon as they enter a room, because they pass on their negative energy to everyone around them. Managers often fail to confront this problem because it comes and goes. Furthermore, these bigger BUTs are more difficult for managers to confront, as there is no easy solution. Ignoring this BUT, however, guarantees that it will not go away. And a bad day for a moody person can result in a bad day for everyone else, particularly those who work closest with that individual.

**THE APB:** The cause of this BUT is personality; Ben is naturally moody. This BUT goes right to the core of who Ben is and how he responds to pressure, conflict, or normal day-to-day work situations. His moodiness manifests itself in negative behaviors like bad-mouthing coworkers or griping about projects, even though the real cause of his bad mood may be rooted in unrelated problems, like a morning traffic setback or the copier's malfunction. These behaviors are the real problem, and though they don't necessarily affect Ben's aptitude for his job, they do affect those around him. Ben's BUT might mean that he will be passed up the next time there's an opportunity for promotion.

**SOLUTION:** If you are that moody person, please get

a handle on your emotions. Take a step back, and have some self-awareness. Realize how your biorhythm roller coaster is negatively impacting the people around you. Try stress-relief exercises like counting, taking deep breaths, or squeezing a stress ball to get rid of those bad vibes in a positive way. If you know that you are having a bad day and you can't control how you are going to react, reschedule your meetings and focus on work you can do alone. A problem is less of a problem if people don't have to experience it firsthand. Manage your emotions, or at least manage your contact with others.

People who are well balanced and can manage the stress and strains of their professional and personal lives are better able to lead. If you are the leader of a team or a manager of others, you have to be extra careful about your mood, because the impact, if negative, can be devastating. Remember when you were a kid and Dad or Mom came home from work in a bad mood? It was not fun for anybody. If you are the team's captain, keep the ship and your mood on an even keel. If you want to manage others, then you'd better get this BUT under control.

---

The key to both finding and managing your BUT is to get a deep understanding of your aptitude, personality, and the triggers that lead to those unwanted behaviors. That deep understanding comes from continuous self-assessment and self-reflection. You have to ask yourself a lot of questions.

Aptitude: What am I good at? What do I enjoy doing?
What activities energize me and make me strong?
What activities drain my energy and undermine my
self-confidence?

Personality: Who am I? What do I value? What do I want?
How do I interact with the world? What type of job
aligns best with my values, wants, needs, and identity?

Behavior: When do I behave in a way that hurts my colleagues or my company? What situations trigger these
negative or destructive responses? Which people in my
company bring out the worst in me? How can I better
predict or avoid these situations so that I am self-aware
and well prepared to deal with them?

When you put an APB out by asking these questions, you
are more likely to find your BUT and the causes of it. By understanding the source, you are better able to predict and manage
the symptoms. The APB approach will also enable you to help
others overcome their weaknesses and shortcomings.

Before you take a new job, you can use the APB framework
to decide if it's really right for you. Study the job requirements
and the group's culture. Then ask yourself this important
question: Is this job a good fit for me? If you discover the job
might conflict with any aspect of your personality or behavior,
then you need to think long and hard about taking it. If the
job is poorly aligned with your aptitude, then your BUT is
going to look really big, really fast. Move on!

## BUT BREAK: ANALYZE THIS!

### "Lauren has a great work ethic, *but* she has weak analytical skills."

You're likely familiar with this funny movie depicting a violent mafia boss seeking therapy. However, there is nothing funny about weak analytical skills if your job requires them. There are a lot of bright, capable people who just don't measure up when it comes to quantitative analysis. In some industries you need to be able to read the charts and crunch the numbers. In other industries, like finance, you need to love the numbers and all the analysis behind them. It's not something you can fake.

**APB:** Lauren wants to get the work done, but she does not have the skills. This has aptitude written all over it.

**SOLUTION:** If you are considering a job that requires intense analysis such as a role in finance, accounting, actuary, etc., make sure your personal toolbox and interests are well aligned. If you have been given feedback that weak analytical skills are your BUT, you should take it very seriously. If you can't do the numbers, you can't do the job. Talk to your manager. Find out what is missing from your tool kit. Will additional training close the gap, or is it a subject-matter aptitude issue? You need to find out. Perhaps there is another great role where your strong interpersonal or project-management skills can be put to good use.

Using the APB can also help you get to the root cause of your BUT—and the cause might not be what you expected it to be. The APB can help you come up with coping strategies for dealing with problems that you can't completely eliminate.

---

### BUT BREAK: ANGER MANAGEMENT
**"Nathan gets the work done, *but* he gets so angry over trivial things."**

We'll date ourselves here by taking you back to the late 1970s with Styx's song "Angry Young Man (Fooling Yourself)." The song is about a guy who has everything going his way, yet, he's always fuming at a world he believes is out to get him.

You are kidding and fooling yourself if you don't believe your angry outbursts are hurting your career and damaging relationships with your colleagues.

Nobody likes an angry man or woman. If you think an apology after an anger outburst sets things right, you are dead wrong. Angry outbursts leave people battered and scarred. People don't like or trust those who are unpredictably explosive. Colleagues will avoid you altogether, or approach you like the U.S. bomb squad soldiers in Iraq approach the explosive-laden car in *The Hurt Locker*. Remember, if you are a time bomb, your company will first defuse you and then dispose of you.

**APB:** This is another BUT rooted in a personality flaw. You might be surprised to learn the cause of this problem may not be a predilection toward anger, but another emotion entirely. We've noticed that most anger, in work or life, is rooted in fear. When people are threatened or worried about their well-being or job security, they will use anger to camouflage their underlying fears. If anger is your problem, fear may be your issue. Instead of asking yourself, "Why am I so angry?" ask yourself, "Why am I so scared?"

**SOLUTION:** Get a grip on your anger and understand your fears. Focus on who or what incites that anger and why. Do everything you can to avoid that person or situation until you identify the true source of the negative emotion. An anger outburst makes you feel better for a minute and makes everyone around you feel bad for a month.

With that said, if you feel an uncontrollable, fear-driven anger attack coming on, remove yourself from the situation. Go to a place far removed from civilization and detonate yourself in private. Then put yourself back together and return to work.

---

Finally, here's an example of a behavioral BUT. This problem afflicts the people who take discussions to places they don't need to go.

---

## BUT BREAK: SINE / COSINE = TANGENT
### "Walter speaks up in meetings,
### *but* then he goes off on tangents."

Our brother Tom likes to call in to Philadelphia talk radio shows.

He has developed an imaginary call-in character named "Sal from the Northeast." Sal always sounds just a little bit off and speaks with a speech impediment. In this world of political correctness, even a nasty or abrupt radio host won't hang up on someone with even the slightest disability. Sal will try to engage the show's host on the issue of the day and keep the one-way conversation going for as long as the host will allow. Sal will tell a personal and seemingly related story on the topic at hand. However, Sal's story purposely has no beginning, has no end, and is riddled with tangential stories that lead absolutely nowhere. Sal speaks with ever-increasing intensity until he builds up and delivers the story's punch line—which also makes no sense whatsoever. Our brother Tom's personal best was an unforgettable eighteen-minute on-air fictional ramble involving Sal from the Northeast and his alleged army buddy, former Philadelphia Eagles football coach Richie Kotite.

Your colleagues are really busy. When a meeting is called to discuss an issue and/or to make a decision, it's critically important that you stay on topic. Bringing up other issues or tangential stories squanders everyone's time and dilutes the focus on the important issue. A table surrounded by high-paid decision makers wastes the firm a lot of money if nothing is decided. Make sure every moment counts. Share your anecdotes or related stories after the work is done.

**APB:** Going off on tangents is a behavior closely related to having very little self-awareness. It's usually a result of liking to hear yourself talk—though even you might not be paying attention to what you're saying.

**SOLUTION:** When speaking in a meeting, stay on topic. Whatever the main issue is, make sure to stick to it. We're sure there are other issues, but everyone in the room wants to resolve the big one. Tangential stories or sub-issues waste time, dilute focus, and distract everyone in the room. Sal from the Northeast, working his magic on an obnoxious and unsuspecting radio host, is funny. Wasting time and company money on subjects or issues of little importance is not.

---

The APB is a simple tool that brings focus to an often elusive BUT problem. Like every other piece of advice provided in this book, the APB approach requires work, focus, and a commitment to self-reflection and self-awareness. Most important, it requires the humility necessary to admit that we are all far from perfect. Once you have all this, you are ready to become a Truth Seeker.

## HANDLING THE TRUTH

No one can forget the famous scene from the film *A Few Good Men* when Jack Nicholson says, "You can't handle the truth." The warning here from us is that if you go searching for the truth about your BUT, you had better make sure you can handle it. Not everyone can.

Right now you are probably saying, "I always ask my boss for feedback," and it's great that you do. However, what really matters is what you do with it. We all love to blame our managers for not giving us enough feedback. Yet, in many cases it's our failure to listen, accept the message, and act on what our manager has told us is the problem. You can't imagine how many times we have given feedback to people who choose to deflect it with a myriad of finger-pointing and excuse making. "You don't understand" is a common refrain from someone who is not ready to handle the truth. This is often followed by a barrage of "ifs" and "ands" so they don't have to accept their BUTs. In the most extreme cases the constructive feedback is met with anger and indignation. Those situations are the most disheartening to a manager and the most destructive to the recipient's career.

If you ask for feedback, accept that feedback earnestly and graciously. Open your heart and mind to the notion that what you are being told is the truth. The person providing it is giving you a valuable gift. That gift can make your life better if you open it and use it. What we lack in self-awareness can be provided to us by caring people who want us to be better than we are. Don't you want to be better than you are?

Still, it's often hard to find your BUT, because many of your peers, as well as your managers, may be afraid to provide truly candid feedback. Therefore, it is critical that you proactively seek out the Truth Tellers in your company to learn and understand what is holding you back. Truth Tellers are people in your professional or personal life who have the courage and candor to tell you the truth about you. It's probably not your direct manager, or you would have found it already.

It's probably not your competitive peers, because they have a vested interest in keeping your BUT hidden from you. It could be a mentor, a friend, a senior executive, or even your assistant. Your spouse is probably familiar with your BUT, though he or she may not know how exposing it at work is negatively impacting your career.

Believe us, there is someone out there who knows your BUT and has the guts to tell you all about it. You must find that Truth Teller and drag the truth out of them. Only then will you discover what's preventing you from getting to the next level. And when you do find out, brace yourself! It's going to hurt.

## THE BUT SLAP

The BUT slap is the moment when people's perception of you suddenly becomes your reality. The image you have of yourself comes crashing down under the weight of how others perceive you. It is, in essence, your moment of truth. If you are fortunate enough to find a Truth Teller to give it to you straight, we want to make sure you are emotionally prepared for what you will be told. We cannot emphasize enough the shock and awe that comes along with a good old-fashioned BUT slap. It can hit you so hard that it loosens your wisdom teeth. If it's a big and ugly BUT you will feel pain right down into your heart and soul. Be forewarned, once your Truth Teller gets started, he or she is not going to hold back.

Here's an example of a BUT that might result in a lighter BUT-slapping session, since it's one that's easier to manage, and therefore easier for your Truth Teller to broach.

## BUT BREAK: MR. FREEZE

### "Vincent is hardworking, *but* he freezes up in a crisis."

You TV and movie junkies will remember the old *Batman* TV series as well as one of the earlier Batman movies, in which Arnold Schwarzenegger played this distinguished villain. The Azelby brothers loved Mr. Freeze. Nobody, however, likes a Mr. or Mrs. Freeze in the office. When confronted with multiple and simultaneous problems, people can shut down. They become paralyzed with fear and they look like Batman after Mr. Freeze has sprayed him with the liquid-ice gun. If there are so many things to be done, these people can seize up and find themselves unable to do anything. Don't allow yourself to become overwhelmed, or colleagues will think you cannot handle the demands that come with more responsibility.

**APB:** The behavior of freezing up is, in most cases, caused by emotions like fear or anxiety. A Mr. Freeze becomes so overwhelmed by the big picture he can't break down the scenario into manageable pieces.

**SOLUTION:** When faced with a multidimensional problem, be cool, but don't freeze up. Break down tasks into smaller steps and pieces and focus on the highest-priority items that you can complete, influence, and/or control. Don't let the larger, uncontrollable issues prevent you from acting decisively and moving forward on the achievable tasks. Think clearly, and act decisively. Just as you never want them to see you sweat, you never want them to see you shiver.

BUTs that have been given time to grow unconstrained become more and more difficult for your Truth Teller to talk about. In the time that it's taken your BUT to grow, you've become so blind to it and its effects that you are in store for the most painful of BUT slaps. The owner of this next BUT will receive a rude awakening when he or she discovers they are not, in fact, their company's repository of knowledge.

---

## BUT BREAK: THE KNOW-IT-ALL

**"Andrew is really bright, *but* he's a know-it-all."**

The *American Idol* winner Kelly Clarkson captures this BUT perfectly in her hit song "Mr. Know It All."

This is the person who must take every opportunity to show the world how much they know about everything. Perhaps you have a know-it-all in your life. Whatever topic is being discussed, they will hijack the conversation and dominate it with their own experiences, articles they have read, or their own self-informed views or opinions. The know-it-all will cut off other speakers or finish their sentences for them. The know-it-all is literally jumping out of his or her skin while you are trying to speak, because they just can't wait to tell the world everything they know. The most annoying habit of the know-it-all is when he or she shakes their head and says, "I know, I know, I know," when you are trying to tell them something important.

**APB:** While the know-it-all believes they are showing the world how smart they are, they're actually highlighting how insecure, selfish, and annoying they are. They are also losing out on the perspectives, knowledge, and experience of those who, in many cases, actually know a lot more than they do. Over time, the know-it-all will become increasingly isolated as their colleagues grow weary of trying to tell them something and repeatedly getting shut down. The flow of information to the know-it-all will eventually cease, putting them at a huge disadvantage to others in the company.

**SOLUTION:** If you are a know-it-all, get over yourself. You don't—and can't possibly—know everything. Please recognize how annoying your BUT is and how it's negatively impacting others' feelings toward you. If you don't value your colleagues' information or opinions, they will stop providing them. Information is the most valuable asset in a company, and your obnoxious behavior will ensure you never receive any.

To help overcome this problem, ask yourself these questions: Why do you feel the need to know everything? What triggers that need? Is it insecurity? Is it a quest for dominance? Are you compensating for something else? Why do you always need to be the smartest person in the room? We're no Sigmund Freuds, so you must figure out what is behind this behavior. Stop trying to be so damn smart. Let the people around you take a turn at being smart. Listen closely to them. Allow them to finish. And most importantly, value their contributions. You'll be surprised by how much they know and by how much you can learn by shutting up and taking notes.

Recall that in Bob's personal BUT-slap session there were two kicks with steel-toe boots delivered. Not only was he a bully, but he was also unappreciative of the people who helped make him and his team successful. Bob could try to shrug off the bully label as "aggressive and determined," but the unappreciative part cut him deeply. He was perceived by some distant colleagues as the jerk that Jack Welch wrote about in his many books on leadership.

Bob's coaching session with his manager reminds us of the 1987 movie *Moonstruck*. Go watch the scene where Cher slaps Nicolas Cage in the face and yells, "Snap out of it!" Watch it closely. She slaps him once to get his attention. Then she delivers a furious second slap with twice the speed, power, and intensity of the first. There is only one thing worse than getting slapped in the face with your own BUT. That is having it done to you twice in rapid succession. However painful, the BUT slap or slaps will enable you to "snap out" of the denial and self-delusion we are all susceptible to.

The bigger your BUT, the bigger your BUT slap. Problems like moodiness and being a know-it-all are destructive to morale, the firm, and your own career. A good manager will confront these behaviors aggressively. Hearing for the first time you are destructive is a painful and eye-opening experience. However, in every single case, the BUT slap is a necessary step on the road to recovery. Bob would have carried his BUT around until the day he was unceremoniously fired had his boss not interceded. (Actually, there would have been a ceremony, but Bob wouldn't have been invited.)

## LISTENING TO YOUR BUT

If a Truth Teller is willing to speak to you about your BUT, you had better listen, and listen closely. You must disarm all of your fight (argue) and flight (deny) instincts and just sit there and take it all in. Listen to what is said, and also listen for important messages that may be too hurtful for your Truth Teller to verbalize but are intimated in other ways. "You need to be more of a team player" can mean "Stop being a self-centered jerk." "Spend more time with your people" can mean "They think you are an arrogant snob." "Step up and take on more" can mean "You're the laziest person on this team." People are generally kind, courteous, and sensitive to your feelings. That's why most of them are lousy Truth Tellers. Great managers and great Truth Tellers care more about your career and the company than they do about your ego and feelings. If you find your Truth Teller, cherish them. When they speak, don't backpedal to the corner and do the "rope a dope." Stand in the middle of the ring with your hands at your side, and absorb every body blow and uppercut that your Truth Teller delivers.

Engage with them. Provoke them. Ask many questions. Request specific examples. Seek clarification. Even if you initially disagree with the Truth Teller's assessment, absorb it fully and accept it at face value. There will be plenty of time later to reconcile what you have just learned. If you allow your fight-or-flight instincts to appear in the Truth-Teller session, you will lose on two fronts. First, the important feedback you should be receiving will be drowned out by your own denials and arguments. These protests are referred to as "reBUTtals," because you are repelling the BUTs that your Truth Teller is imparting on you. Second, your pushback may indicate you can't take constructive feedback or that you have no interest in improving your performance. Hearing what your BUT is and taking responsibility for it is the only way you can own it and manage it. It's like a drug intervention or the twelve-step AA program. You first have to recognize and admit you have a problem before you can actually fix the problem. The biggest risk associated with not accepting your BUT is that the people around will give up on you. Who wants to work with someone who refuses to acknowledge or fix a problem they have been told is a problem?

This form of denial reminds us of getting pulled over for speeding. Our dad was a New York City cop, therefore we have been trained for such situations. First off, never say, "What seems to be the problem, Officer?" This makes you sound like a pompous jerk who is pretending to be polite. Also, if you tell the radar-gun-holding police officer you were not speeding, you are basically telling him that he's an idiot. That is a bad way to start your relationship. Instead, first acknowledge that you must have been doing something wrong or you would not have been pulled over. It's your best hope of getting off with a warning. The same is true of Truth Tellers. If they care enough to take the effort and "pull you over" at work, you have to accept the fact that you are doing something wrong.

Why do people sabotage themselves and ignore the important information from their Truth Teller? We ask ourselves this every time we see it happen. By protecting their egos, people destroy their potential. As you will see below, if your BUT is being an obstructionist, the only thing you will stop is your own advancement. The fact is, some people desperately want to maintain the status quo. Don't be one of them.

---

## BUT BREAK: THE BPU

### "Peter gets high grades for risk management, *but* he's an obstructionist."

A BPU is a member of the Business Prevention Unit. These are the people who feel the world is a static place and what is successful today will also be successful tomorrow. A BPU is heavily invested and empowered in the present. They don't want change because it may weaken their power base. Therefore, they believe everything new is too risky to try because it introduces risk to them if the company changes. BPUs are the reason that companies always get slower as they get bigger.

We are sure you have some of these people in your company. There are a few surgically implanted into every organization. They sit on management, control, risk, or compliance committees although they may have no expertise in these areas. Sometimes they just sit in the gallery waiting to pounce on or sabotage any attempts at creativity or a new approach. They do their very best to kill any original idea that diverges from the normal course of business.

Raising concerns and assessing the risks of new ventures are part of any robust new product– or initiative-approval process. It's important to have experienced committee members who oversee this important function. The advocate for a new initiative must be fully prepared to overcome all objections with facts and a detailed assessment of both the manageable and the uncontrollable risks. The challenge with BPUs is they often resort to scare tactics and raise concerns or issues that are difficult to quantify or deflect. They use ominous terms like "business risk," "reputation risk," "franchise risk," "regulatory risk," or "litigation risk" to scare the hell out of everyone in the room. The BPU trots out these terms whenever a change in the business model is being discussed. They are used in an attempt to paralyze the decision-making body. Sometimes this scare tactic works, and sometimes it does not. Either way, these fear-mongering terms create a time-consuming and energy-wasting roadblock.

If the advocates for change and the decision-making body are able to overcome the BPU's alarmist concerns and approve the new venture, then the BPU employs his or her next favorite tactic. The BPU starts to write himself or herself "I-told-you-so" call options. The BPU will never, ever provide any public support for a new initiative. Instead the BPU will tell everyone they are "very concerned" and they warned the committee this will end badly. We suspect the BPU secretly hopes the new initiative will fail miserably, because the BPU would much rather say, "I told you so," than see the new initiative succeed.

Big companies are a magnet and breeding ground for BPUs, who are born with a roll of red tape in their mouths. BPUs suck the energy out of the people trying to improve and grow the business. Working with a BPU is like driving your car with the parking brake on. And, like parking brakes, BPUs have to be released as soon as you know they are the problem. Remember, talented people want to work with colleagues who can help them move the business forward. We are not advocating speeding. However, if you do not identify and remove your BPUs, your company will be stuck in neutral.

**APB:** The BPU is not generally an aptitude issue, although we have met a few where you scratch your head and say, what does he or she do? What talents do they have? What value have they ever created? Who exactly do they have pictures of? The BPU's personality is the root of their problem. BPUs are fearful. They were probably born that way or became that way early in life. The unknown breeds fear in them, and change introduces the unknown. The BPU wants the world and their role in it to stay exactly the same. It's fear of change that leads to the obstructionist behaviors. It also diminishes their aptitude, because they never try new things—and as a result they learn very little.

**SOLUTION:** Ask yourself, "Might I be a member of the Business Prevention Unit?" This is a BUT that may be limiting your advancement and annoying your colleagues. What you believe is a healthy dose of skepticism may be perceived by others as obstruction. What you believe is discipline and caution may be perceived as rigidity and insecurity. What you believe is focus may be perceived by others as a lack of innovation and motivation. To shrink this BUT, you must be open to new ideas. Explore potential innovations with energy and enthusiasm and look for ways to make them work. Try some new things. Take some risk.

Change can be frightening because of the uncertainty, but it's necessary for successful businesses. The status quo and the Business Prevention Unit are doomed for extinction. Don't be part of either.

---

When receiving feedback from your Truth Teller, first acknowledge there must be truth in the feedback and you are committed to improving in this area of development. Nothing makes a Truth Teller feel more encouraged and optimistic about the potential for positive change than hearing someone accept the feedback provided and he or she is committed to self-improvement. And nothing angers a Truth Teller more than being dismissed as not knowing what they are talking about, even when they are holding indisputable evidence. People who dismiss or ignore the Truth Teller do so at their own peril.

After you've received your BUT slap, you can pay it forward, too. A good Truth Teller speaks openly and honestly about his or her own BUTs before delivering a BUT slap. This acknowledgment of the Truth Teller's own weaknesses creates an environment of both trust and receptivity with the person who is about to receive their difficult message. The Truth Teller should provide as much detail as possible about not only their BUTs but also how they became aware of them. Who was their Truth Teller? How were they impacted by the news? How did they respond? Where are they now on these issues? It's also extremely important the Truth Teller express gratitude for their Truth Teller. This will help ensure the message is received as caring and instructive feedback, jarring as it may be. It also increases the likelihood that today's BUT-slap recipient will become tomorrow's Truth Teller.

## THE SECOND OPINION

As described earlier, when the person you believe to be your Truth Teller confronts you with your BUT, you must be open-minded and self-reflective. However, Truth Tellers, like doctors, don't always nail the diagnosis. Sometimes they get it wrong, which means you should always seek a second opinion. After you have been armed with the initial BUT diagnosis, go meet with other Truth Tellers, colleagues, and friends to see if they concur with the original assessment. They may or may not. Either way, it's incredibly important you complete the due diligence on yourself.

Our friend Paul is an extremely successful private equity investor. Earlier in his career, the CEO of his company told Paul he was good at execution *but* had no strategic vision. At that stage of Paul's career he was primarily focused on managing and integrating companies. At first, Paul was stung by that assessment and took those words to heart. However, with some time, effort, and the insights of his colleagues, mentors, and other industry professionals, he came to realize his boss was flat-out wrong. Paul critically assessed himself and asked others with whom he had worked to provide feedback on his strengths and weaknesses. Paul's vision and strategy were rated as strongly as his execution. Paul's boss fancied himself as the visionary, strategic thinker, and since Paul was doing all of the heavy lifting, integrating the portfolio companies, he was cast as an "execution guy." Fortunately, Paul never accepted the diagnosis and sought many other opinions. He examined his own aptitude, behavior, and personality for his job (there's that APB again!) and reached a very different conclusion. Today he's one of the great strategic thinkers across multiple sectors of the private equity industry.

If you receive a diagnosis you believe is inaccurate, go get a second or third opinion. The key is self-awareness; Paul listened to his Truth Teller, considered his BUT slap, and examined his performance to come to the conclusion that this particular BUT did not belong to him. BUTs are serious business. An incorrect diagnosis can lead to improper treatment. You, the patient, will be far worse off if you don't get a second opinion.

Like we said, BUTs *are* serious business, but don't get carried away . . .

---

## BUT BREAK: WHY SO SERIOUS?
### "Kevin is a great accountant, *but* he needs to lighten up."

"Why so serious?" These are the haunting words uttered by Heath Ledger as the Joker in *The Dark Knight*. It's a question that some intense, uptight, and humorless employees need to hear. Watching someone's pulsating carotid artery and bulging temple veins as they breathlessly describe the challenges of the technology upgrade initiative does not inspire confidence and leaves people feeling both nervous and exhausted. What a "stress machine" considers passion and commitment is received by colleagues as a stroke waiting to happen. Unless you are a trained paramedic, do you really want to spend time with someone who is wound up this tight?

**APB:** Your tight BUT, in this case, is not from the squats you do at the gym. It is part of your personality. You are a very serious person and you take your job, and yourself, perhaps a little too seriously. You may not display bad behaviors, but you are probably lacking some good ones. Greeting people with a smile and a "good morning" is a desired behavior. Saying "please" and "thank you" to the people who help you is a good behavior. Lightening up a tension-filled conference room with a funny comment is also a desired behavior. And you don't have to be Chris Rock to do any of them.

**SOLUTION:** Lighten up. We are not doing brain surgery here, and we are not in a Higgins boat landing on Omaha Beach on 6/6/44. We are simply delivering products and services to customers. Making a reasonable profit is not a life-or-death exercise. You can smile once in a while and engage a colleague in conversation that has nothing to do with the bottom line. Take down the intensity a few notches, and the work will still get done. Athletes and workers who are focused and relaxed play better and work better than those who are nervous and stressed.

# THE FIVE STAGES OF PROCESSING YOUR BUT

In her 1969 book *On Death and Dying*, Elisabeth Kübler-Ross describes the five stages of grief that people with a terminal diagnosis go through before they leave this world.

1.  Denial: they refuse to believe they are dying.
2.  Anger: they get mad at God or life in general for their situation.
3.  Bargaining: they begin to negotiate with God or with themselves for more time.
4.  Depression: they are sullen and sad about their impending death.
5.  Acceptance: they accept the fact they are dying and they are at peace with it.

Granted, your BUT is not likely to kill you. However, it can certainly sicken your career if it's not diagnosed and treated quickly. If you put a lot of effort into your job and you care deeply about it, getting a harsh BUT diagnosis will hurt you emotionally and in extreme cases physically. You will go through these five stages when your Truth Teller divulges your ailment. The bigger your BUT, the more time it will take to go through these stages.

Let's suppose Terri, your manager, calls you into her office unexpectedly. You are working on a big project with the strategy group, so you guess she wants an update. Terri shuts the door behind you and tells you to sit down. Terri says, "Gerard, I just got off a conference call with the strategy group, and they told me you are not being a team player. They said you are not cooperating, you are being defensive, and they have to pry information out of you. I have noticed these behaviors myself, and they need to be corrected."

Gerard is both stunned and hurt by the strategy group's assessment and his manager's concurrence. He now has to process this information. Gerard may work his way through the Kübler-Ross model in the following way:

Denial: "This is total BS. I'm not like that."

Anger: "Now *Terri* is out to get me. I bet it was Jenny in the strategy group who was behind all of this. I'm calling her out, and then I'm resigning."

Bargaining: "I can't resign. What am I going to tell my wife? My oldest daughter is going to college, and my son is getting braces. I need this job. I'll sit tight for now and start looking around."

Depression: "This is hopeless. I've got fifteen years invested in this place, and everyone thinks I'm a jerk. I am going to hide in my cubicle and mind my own business."

Acceptance: "Okay, so maybe I was not supportive of this project in the first place. Yes, I probably was defensive because this project only had downside for me. Maybe I can work on these issues and turn this thing around. I'm here, so I might as well try to fix it."

When the Truth Teller, in this example Terri, confronts you with your BUT it's only natural that you work your way through these five stages. Our suggestion is you do this as quickly and quietly as possible. If you stay too long in either the denial or depression stage, it will be evident to everyone around you, and it will set you back further. Also, if you walk around as a highly visible and vocal malcontent you are asking for even more trouble. If your goal is to be fired, do the denial and anger thing in a big way, and we're sure you'll be successful.

If you go on arguing with your Truth Teller, or anyone else, for that matter, you won't last long.

---

## BUT BREAK: THE ARGUER
### "I appreciate Susan for her strong opinions, *but* she is so argumentative."

Growing up in northern New Jersey we were all Yankee fans. Joe and Tom (aka Sal from the Northeast) were actually vendors at Yankee Stadium in the late 1970s, so we were all definitely familiar with Billy Martin. He was the Yankees' manager, and perhaps the greatest arguer of all time. When an umpire made a close or questionable call that went against the Yankees, Billy Martin would come sprinting out of the dugout and get right up in the umpire's face. He would turn his baseball cap sideways so he could get his face even closer, and his mouth would explode in a tirade of expletives mixed with saliva. The umpire would go nose to nose with Billy and then throw him out of the game. Billy also loved to argue with Yankee owner George Steinbrenner, who hired and fired Billy on five different occasions.

People who love to argue approach every disagreement as a full-contact sport. The Arguer feels if someone has a view that is different from their own, then that view and its owner must be summarily destroyed. The Arguer will keep attacking until the other person submits to an unconditional surrender of their opinion. The Arguer views every discussion as a winner-take-all war of words. They want to knock out their opponent, stand over the prone and lifeless body, and raise their arms victoriously in the air. If you are the undefeated Arguer in your office, we want you to know nobody is keeping score. Nobody "gives a rat's behind" (our dad's favorite expression) that you were captain of your high school debate team.

Here's a little heads-up for the Arguer. Issues can be discussed without an argument. People can disagree without attacking each other. The strength of the reasoning behind a position is more powerful than the loud voice or the aggressive lean in across the conference table. Your "let's start an argument" act is probably growing old in the office. People have gotten wise to you and no longer include you when important things need to be discussed. If you argue aggressively and inappropriately with colleagues, perhaps you'll do the same with clients. And that's just not good for business. People who argue too often or too aggressively get thrown out of games and ultimately get fired.

**APB:** Incessant arguing is a personality flaw that leads to aggressive behaviors that offend people. Billy Martin had a creative baseball mind. He won a lot of games and the World Series in 1977. Aptitude was not his issue. He got fired five times because everyone, including the Boss, got tired of his antics. Don't be a Billy Martin.

**SOLUTION:** If you work with someone who loves to argue, here are a couple of thoughts. Arguers love to bait the trap with an emotion-evoking comment. Don't take the bait. Our good friend Kevin, who is an expert in negotiations and human nature, refers to these provocative comments or emails as "pitches in the dirt." His advice is always the same: "Don't swing at them!"

The other adage to keep in mind: "If you argue with a fool, after thirty seconds nobody knows who is who." So don't give the Arguer what he or she is looking for. Engagement with them only cheapens you.

If you are the Arguer, tone it down a few notches. Get rid of the anger. Turn off the emotion and turn on the reason. Discussions are much more fruitful than arguments, because people can't listen when they are arguing. And you can't learn anything if you are not listening. Business is not a winner-take-all game. Compromise is a perfectly acceptable and often more viable outcome. And yes, good friends and valuable colleagues are allowed to disagree with you.

---

Once you have quickly worked your way through the five stages, it's time to get back to work and start kissing your BUT good-bye. Okay, you are disappointed in yourself, and yes, this is a setback. At least you now know what you have suspected for some time. Your career has been going sideways. You have not been the go-to person in your unit for quite some time. Your attitude has been a lingering issue. It took this project and a Truth Teller like Terri to finally drag your BUT out of the darkness and into the light. You have now received the message. It knocked you down and rattled your brains. Now that you have processed it and accepted it, it's time to fix it. That takes both hard work and determination, and you have plenty of both. It's time to get your BUT up off the canvas and start fighting back.

## THE PAIN OF CHANGE

People can go through their entire careers without ever realizing their BUT is causing them tremendous pain. While they may not feel the pain, they definitely experience the other symptoms. They say ignorance is bliss, but is it really? Perhaps you are no longer the go-to person when a problem arises. The peer to whom you always compared yourself gets promoted and you don't. The less experienced person in the adjacent cubicle gets assigned the big project. The person you trained a few years back gets lifted out of your department for a big job in another area. You are frustrated that you are being overlooked, but you blame it on politics, an incompetent manager, bad chemistry, or corporate dysfunction. There is a reason you are not moving forward, and that reason is you. Denial and delusion are like anesthesia for the ego. They are wonderful masking agents that allow people to accept disappointment after disappointment without ever looking within themselves to find the source of these failures.

Learning what your BUT is can be very painful. Understanding how your BUT has held you back brings that pain to life. Think of the days, months, and years that you did not capitalize on opportunity because you lacked the self-awareness to find the issue that was holding you back. That is a painful lesson now learned. You need to stop masking that pain and embrace it thoroughly. That pain lays the groundwork for change.

People do not like pain, and they do not like change. The two are closely related. People change when the pain of staying the same is greater than the pain of change. Only when you understand you have been enduring the tremendous pain of the status quo will you take on the pain involved in changing. Your BUT is the source of these failures, and yet you choose to ignore it. Why? Is your ego so fragile you cannot accept that, like every human being, you are flawed? Acknowledging and accepting your BUT is a humbling process. Managing your BUT is hard work. In the U.S. Marine Corps, young men and women at basic-training boot camp are told by drill instructors, "Pain is weakness leaving the body."

Think about that for a minute. You have a weakness, and we call it a BUT. Make no mistake about it: if you want to conquer your BUT, the process will be painful. It will take a long time and an enormous amount of work to get that weakness to leave your body. U.S. Marine Corps boot camp training lasts for twelve weeks. Young men and women leave there physically and mentally stronger than ever. Your personal "BUT camp" will take much longer. Are you one of the few? Are you one of the proud? Can you handle the truth and the pain of your BUT leaving your body? We'll find out, won't we?

Don't fear changing. Only fear what will happen if you don't. If your BUT happens to be based in fear, then you'll have to work extra hard at this.

---

## BUT BREAK: CAPE FEAR

### "Sandra knows what needs to be done, *but* she just can't pull the trigger."

Unlike indecisiveness, with fearfulness you actually know what you need to do but you are simply afraid to do it. You obsess over the things that might go wrong if you act, rather than the things that will improve when you take action. If you are seen as fearful or insecure, senior management will be reluctant to give you more responsibility. An inability to act is an inability to lead. People will not follow someone into battle who has fear in his or her eyes. Business and life are about taking action to fix problems. One is always better off making and implementing decisions on problems than just standing still. Problems do not age well, so move forward and deal with them right now!

In World War II, Germany was the problem. General George Patton always had his Third Army on the attack moving toward and through Germany. Only audacity and more audacity would break the spirit of a well-trained and equipped German army.

Patton knew a moving army is more aggressive, more confident, and has better morale than a standing army. Attack your business problems and watch your team's success and morale soar.

**APB:** Fearfulness and failure to act can be a dangerously potent cocktail of APB. If you have never faced a particular type of business problem, you may not feel you have the aptitude to manage it. If so, go ask for the help of someone who has dealt with it before. Fearfulness or a lack of confidence can be part of your personality. Perhaps you were born fearful, or you had overbearing parents who contributed to your fearfulness and lack of self-confidence. Either way you have to manage that fear on your own or seek professional help. Lastly, the behavior part of this fear-based BUT will almost always be procrastination. Yes, you can always face your fear tomorrow. But remember, problems do not age well. They only get bigger when left unattended.

**SOLUTION:** If you receive development feedback on your fear to act you had better act on it quickly. We suggest you have a conversation with your boss and tell him or her you understand your failure to take action is hurting the organization. Make it clear you will improve on this issue or leave the firm. This will force you to put it all on the line, and you will have no other choice but to act when required. This is a much better plan—and one with infinitely more potential for success—than putting your tail between your legs and waiting around for them to come for you.

---

There's no way around it. Meeting your BUT face-to-face is a painful ordeal. But *not* dealing with your BUT can lead to even more pain and suffering. Take Bob's experience as proof that dealing with your problems means fixing your problems.

Bob worked as the VP of sales for a small medical management company, and he knew his boss, the CEO, was not happy with his performance. The company was poorly managed and was in disarray. Bob was quite certain he was on the verge of being fired when the CEO brought in a co-VP of sales. At first Bob was mad and felt sorry for himself. He sulked in his office for a couple of weeks. He was also miserable at home. Here he was in a new city with his wife and newborn baby, and he was about to get fired. He was asking himself, "Just how bad am I?"

At the same time this was going on, Bob was leading a cross-functional team focused on improving the company's operations. One morning, Bob woke up from his self-induced, feeling-sorry-for-himself coma and realized he knew more about the company than anyone else in the organization, including his CEO. Bob finally decided he no longer cared about the prospect of being fired, and he was simply embarrassed about how he had become consumed and paralyzed by the idea of losing his job. The day of reckoning had arrived. Bob knew he needed to lay it on the line with his boss and let the future play out.

Bob walked into the boss's office and told him what the company needed, and that for the company to be successful, his boss needed to step back and let the team execute. At the end of the knock-down, drag-out argument, Bob was the new COO.

His courage to confront the boss in hand-to-hand combat over the future of the company paid off. His boss finally recognized that Bob was right and gave him more responsibility.

To this day, Bob is still disgusted with himself for feeling sorry for himself for so long. He always knew what had to be done, but he was fearful of the consequences. Overcoming his fear and taking aggressive action provided the greatest learning experience he has ever had in his career. He will never again be afraid to lose his job. That specific life experience is liberating and necessary for long-term success. Make no mistake about it: there will be times in your career when you have to be willing to put your job on the line. Just ask yourself, "If the outcome I fear happens, can I live with it?" If the answer is yes, then do what needs to be done.

The sooner you get to the acceptance of your BUT the sooner you'll fix it. Everyone has a BUT or two, so you should not feel so special. Don't deny it. Don't get angry. Don't start bargaining or rationalizing. Don't get bummed out. If you have to go through the Kübler-Ross model, do it quickly so you can get on with accepting and fixing your problem.

## UNDERSTANDING YOUR BUT AND ITS ORIGIN

Once your BUT has been exposed to you, it's critically important you stare at it and fully understand it. You need to think back about your life and your career and try to figure out when it first appeared and the reasons for it. You have to ask yourself, "Why am I doing these things?" Your BUT could be genetic.

Perhaps one or both of your parents have a similar BUT. Just as Lady Gaga sings, "Baby I was born this way!" your BUT could be deeply embedded in the forty-six chromosomes your parents gave to you.

Your BUT could also be the result of some long-since-past personal or professional event that helped to shape it. Perhaps something happened that made you vow never to let it happen again. So today you overcompensate to avoid reopening an old wound. Your BUT could be due to something you are currently struggling with at work or at home. It may now be affecting how you interact with others at work. Maybe your business unit is struggling, and you are feeling the pressure. Perhaps your wife wants a divorce or one of your children is sick. All of that pain and worry is being brought to work and changing how people see you.

We are not geneticists or psychologists, but there is probably an explanation for why you act the way you do. Try to identify the issues influencing your actions. You need to do a full 360-degree review of your BUT. You need to understand its origin and fully appreciate the impact it is having on you, your subordinates, peers, customers, and your manager. You need to look at your BUT from their angle and perspective to fully assess the damage it has caused. Using the APB can help you not only identify your BUT; it can also help you determine its origin. If it's an aptitude-related BUT, maybe you should have taken a particular undergraduate class instead of testing out of it, or maybe you do really need to attend next year's training seminar. If your BUT is personality-based, then look into those nature-or-nurture reasons in your genes and your past that might be creating some problems for you now. And if your BUT is behavior-based, then figure out what the triggers for those behaviors are and try to understand why those things are triggers in the first place.

Let's look at the next BUT with the lens of context. This is a very common BUT that can be fixed by knowing your own limitations.

---

## BUT BREAK: FINISH! FIRST

**"Katie works hard, *but* she stretches herself too thin."**

All three of Joe's daughters played high school basketball. A couple of years ago, Joe noticed that if you wanted to sound like a dad who knew a lot about basketball, you just scream out the word "Finish!" whenever one of the girls drives the lane but misses the layup. (Apparently, if you yell, "Finish!" as loudly and as aggressively as you can, this certifies your in-depth knowledge of basketball.) Why a middle-aged man feels the need to chide and embarrass a sixteen-year-old girl for missing a layup is the topic for another book. We can tell you one thing: the yelling only increases the probability that she misses the next one.

In the business world, it is critically important to finish all of the projects and tasks you have been assigned. Business is all about delivering a high-quality finished product to customers at a good price. That's how companies like Target and Amazon win over customers. Within a company, your colleagues are your customers. You must build a personal brand of delivering high-quality work in the shortest amount of time possible. Time is the currency of companies, and you want to use it as effectively and efficiently as possible, while always maintaining high quality. Finish the task at hand before starting the next one. Overreaching leads to shoddy work and late delivery. Both will destroy your personal brand. Trust us, the last thing you need is a middle-aged man aggressively yelling "Finish!" at you over the top of your cubicle.

**APB:** This BUT is caused by its owner taking on too much responsibility. This is a behavior that can be caused by a lack of aptitude (you can't actually get the work done) or by a personality trait (you don't want to seem needy and ask for help or seem weak and say you don't have time). Perhaps this BUT developed because of its owner's insecurity about not delivering the same quantity of work as some of his or her coworkers. Unfortunately, in trying to match their colleagues' prolificacy, their quality of work has begun to suffer as well.

**SOLUTION:** The best way to prevent this BUT from growing is having the courage to say no. Some people have trouble staying focused on the highest priorities when people show up asking for help. Check in with your manager to stay on top of his or her top priorities. And don't be swayed by a needy colleague seeking your help with something else. Stay focused on the highest-priority task at hand and say "no," or at least "later," to all other requests before you've done a great job with what's already on your plate.

Joe has struggled with this BUT for years and has come to terms with it, not only because he has accepted his Truth Teller's wisdom, but because he has also figured out some of its root causes.

---

## BUT BREAK: PROJECT MYOPIA
### "Joe is aggressive and determined, *but* he doesn't consider the views of others."

We chose the name Joe for this one, because he himself has a case of Project Myopia. Once Joe gets an idea in his head and he mentally commits to pursue it, he tends to dismiss or minimize the views and concerns voiced by others. The more challenging and ambitious the project, the more he tends to block out negative energy created by opposing views. He has been told in his 360-degree reviews this is an important development area for him. His colleagues on various management committees get frustrated with him when he gets into that hyperfocused and determined state of mind needed to launch a new initiative. Their view is that he mentally and emotionally commits to a project way too soon. They want him to be more paced and measured in his assessments. He also needs to invite and consider all of the insights, concerns, and risks his very experienced peers raise.

**APB:** In this case the main concern is aptitude. New products and new markets pose a host of new risks and challenges. Success in one product or market does not guarantee success in another. While self-confidence is a great personality trait to have, it can magnify the bad outcomes associated with a lack of aptitude or experience in a certain area. The behaviors that can come into play in Project Myopia are impatience, stubbornness, and an unwillingness to listen to the concerns of others. The A, P, and B all need to be managed carefully in a case of Project Myopia.

**SOLUTION:** The best way to manage Project Myopia is to argue the opposing view of your great strategic or tactical recommendation before taking it to others. Joe tends to fall in love with his ideas like a tween-aged girl falls for the latest young heart-throb. The more unique, interesting, and challenging the idea is, the harder he falls for it. Before you go into that conference room and make a complete fool of yourself in front of your management committee, make sure you have considered and neutralized the many objections that all new ideas must overcome. If there are risks that cannot be eliminated or managed, then they must be discussed as such, and the case must be made that those risks are worth taking. The ability to discuss vigorously both for and against any recommendation will help you make better decisions. It will also highlight to your colleagues that you take a thoughtful and balanced approach to your risk taking and decision making. Your final recommendation should include all objections and counterviews. They should be highlighted and catalogued so that everyone involved feels they had a voice and contributed to the process. Listen to and leverage the experiences of the talented people around you. They just might save you from doing something really stupid.

Joe has been working on his myopic-minded BUT and feels

he is making progress. He is more balanced when he brings new ideas to the table. He is more clinical and less emotional in his presentation style. He highlights the risks early in the discussion, before others raise them for him. He has learned risks highlighted by the project advocate are far less concerning to managers than risks raised by others. It simply shows the presenter has considered and assessed the risk and remains an advocate.

(Now that we have finished patting Joe on the back, it's time to divulge that in the writing of this book Joe's Project Myopia BUT was in full display on more than a few occasions. He has largely focused on the content writing, and Bob has overseen the editing. Joe consistently and repeatedly dismissed Bob's objections and counterviews. Bob's editing suggestions were met by Joe's defensiveness and stubbornness. Luckily, Bob is also an aggressive advocate of his opinions and he has the will and stamina to wear Joe down until the right answer is found and accepted. Bob's persistence has made this book readable and reminded Joe that BUTs have a tendency to reappear.)

---

**Wrap-up:** Staring at your BUT can be a revealing and unpleasant exercise. If your BUT is really big you are going to be embarrassed and upset by it. Like all other challenges and setbacks in life, you will adjust to it. Trust us, each day it will get a little easier to look at.

Understanding *why* your BUT is there is the easiest way to learn to accept it. Your BUT is simply a function of who you are, what your life journey has taught you, or a reflection of what you are dealing with currently. Now that the shock and horror of studying every last blemish on your BUT has passed, it's time that you accept it for what it is. The human condition is imperfect, and so are many great business leaders of past and present like Henry Ford, Bill Gates, Warren Buffett, and Steve Jobs. Whether your BUT is very large or very small, it will never completely go away, because at its very core it is part of who you are. Like an alcohol- or drug-dependent person who is genetically, physically, and psychologically vulnerable to their addictions, you too run the risk of that BUT reappearing if you lose focus. However, by discovering, staring at, and most importantly, accepting it and its origin, you can begin to manage it, control it, and master it. Think about how long you have been dragging your BUT around without even knowing how big it was. Think about how it has been slowing you down. It's time to pick your BUT up off the ground and start running again.

# CHAPTER 3

# BOUNCING OFF YOUR BUT

**N**ever forget that setbacks and disappointments are part of life and business careers. Throughout your working life you will have bad outcomes or receive feedback that will cut you deep or knock you down. You have to get over and recover from the bad things in business and in life.

According to Confucius, "Our greatest glory is not in never falling, but in rising every time we fall."

---

## BUT BREAK: RAGING BULL
### "Christopher survived the turmoil of the financial crisis, *but* he has shown no resiliency since."

We will never forget the scene in *Raging Bull* in which a bloodied and battered Jake LaMotta, with his eyes almost swollen shut, screams repeatedly at his victorious opponent, Sugar Ray Robinson, " Never got me down, Ray!" LaMotta obviously lost the fight, but he remained proud, defiant, and determined despite the outcome. If Sugar Ray Robinson had knocked him down, the "Raging Bull" LaMotta would have gotten up. Resiliency is all about getting back up.

The same is true in business. Apple is a terrific example of a company that got up off the mat. Apple was getting the hell beat out of it in the 1990s and almost lost its franchise. They were down for the count when a defiant Steve Jobs returned to the company that fired him. He chided his colleagues to get up off the mat and start fighting back against the forces that were driving Apple out of business. With an unmatched combination of creativity, focus, guile, and will, Apple today is the undisputed heavyweight champion and one of the most valuable companies in the world.

**SOLUTION:** When you get knocked down with career setbacks or harsh but true feedback, you too need to bounce back up. The emotional beating you take in a crushing loss or a BUT-slap meeting is both a wake-up call and an opportunity. Your short-term response to adversity will determine the long-term outcome of your career. Get up!

---

We'll share another story with you about coauthor Bob that will illustrate the power of resiliency.

## THE CHAMP NEEDS A KNOCKOUT

In the summer of 1976 the sport of boxing entered the Azelby home. It was an Olympic year, and Sugar Ray Leonard won his gold medal in Montreal. Our middle brother Tommy was twelve years old and that previous November had joined the boxing program run by the Dumont Recreation Department. Every Wednesday night he would go down to the old Borough Hall building and spar with other young aspiring pugilists. Tommy had white-blond hair, big blue eyes, and an innocent, angelic face.

He was undersized for his age, and boys who did not know him often made the mistake of choosing him as a sparring partner. "Whitey," as he came to be known, was a fearless and proficient boxer with lightning-quick hands. He delivered powerful combinations that put larger kids on their butts soon after the opening bell rang. Boys that underestimated the little blond-haired kid paid a high price for their overconfidence.

In the basement of our home, Tommy set up his own boxing ring, where he looked to hone his skills and further develop his love for the sport. An old clothesline that wrapped around the basement's support columns and weaved through the railing of the cellar steps was Whitey's own Madison Square Garden Felt Forum. A boxer who was felled in this ring did not fall to a padded canvas, but rather to a concrete floor painted battle-ship gray. We owned two sets of boxing gloves but could not afford the protective headgear. So if the punch did not knock you out, the floor just might. Tommy would invite neighbor-hood kids and friends over to spar. However, after their first experience in the dungeon ring with Whitey they never re-turned for a second fight. Word quickly spread throughout the neighborhood of the violence and carnage in the Azelby basement. Tommy could no longer find a willing sparring partner.

## ENTER "RAGING CALF"

In an act of desperation, Tommy lured our youngest brother, Bobby, then eight years old, to be his sparring partner. Bobby was of average size, very athletic, and had acquired, at an early age, a tenacious competitive streak that helped ensure his survival. To lure Bobby into the ring, Tommy had to concoct an elaborate set of rules to convince Bobby he could survive and perhaps even win the proposed fight.

The rules were set up as follows: It was a three-round, Olympic-style bout with each round lasting three minutes. The critical rule that Tommy developed to get Bobby into the ring was that Tommy could not punch back until the final minute of the last round. Any blow delivered by Tommy prior to the final minute of the third round would result in immediate disqualification and young Bobby would be declared the victor.

In their first match young Bobby approached his older brother with extreme caution, in the event Tommy forgot the rules. Bobby began throwing punches as Tommy danced around the ring, covering up his face or bobbing and weaving his head to avoid Bobby's punches. Other times Tommy would lean back on the ropes, cover up, and rope-a-dope as young Bobby gleefully flailed away. Bobby would search for an opening between Tommy's gloves in the hopes of landing a face punch. Tommy would chide and encourage Bobby by repeatedly screaming, "The champ is in serious trouble!!!"

With a minute to go in the third and final round, Tommy would lower his gloves and announce, "The champ needs a knockout to win!" This was the signal to young Bobby that his little world was about to take a turn for the worse. Bobby would stop punching and immediately cover his face with his gloves and prepare for the barrage of punches that were about to come. As quick as a flash, Tommy's left jab would split Bobby's gloves and a straight right hand to the face would knock Bobby to the concrete floor. Dazed and confused, Bobby would take all of the ten-second count to get back up and prepare for the next onslaught. Tommy's left jab followed by the straight right hand would again do the trick, and Bobby was back on the floor. Now with only twenty seconds remaining, all Bobby had to do was stay on his feet and avoid the third knockdown and the technical knockout (TKO). The egg timer on the washing machine was ticking down, and Bobby desperately waited for the timer bell to signal his victory. It was not to be. As Bobby lowered his head and groped blindly to grab Tommy's arms to tie him up, a vicious uppercut snapped Bobby's head upward and knocked him to the floor for a third time. Tommy raised his arms in celebration as Bobby sat dejected on the floor with tears in his eyes from the uppercut to the nose and blotchy red cheeks from the straight right-hands.

If this brutal event was not enough for the four Azelby children to be put in foster homes, then the many fights that followed should have been. Young Bobby climbed into that ring many times with his older brother Tommy. Bobby always fought bravely and each time believed he could win. It was not to be. Each time Tommy declared, "The champ needs a knockout to win!" it was soon delivered. Never once did Bobby quit, and never once did he fail to get back up on his feet. He lost time and time again in the final seconds of the final round.

Business is much like boxing. You take some big punches during your career and at times you will find yourself on the canvas, or in the case of the Azelby home, on the concrete floor. Resiliency is the ability to pick yourself up and continue fighting even against the most daunting odds. The next time you have a setback at work and you feel like quitting, think about that eight-year-old boy in the New Jersey basement who never gave up and always got up.

## WHIPPING YOUR BUT

You can't fool people when it comes to fixing your BUT. They will see right through a token effort or the slightest insincerity regarding the steps you are taking to fix the problem. You are better off not trying than faking it. The commitment to change must come from deep within you if you are to sell it to those who have suffered from your BUT for so long. It will take focus, effort, stamina, and a commitment to exercising the weak muscles underlying your BUT. Shrinking your BUT is all about checking your ego at the door and making a sincere and concerted effort to be an effective professional and a better partner and employee. You can do it if you really want to!

To whip your BUT you don't need any special tools or equipment. All you need is a higher level of self-awareness than you have ever had before. You have been put on notice by your Truth Teller. You have studied and accepted your BUT. You have announced publicly you are committed to shrinking your BUT. Now it's your turn to focus exclusively on it and whip it into shape. To do that you must accept the fact that while you can exercise your BUT you will never completely exorcise your BUT. A priest will not come to your house and expel it à la Linda Blair. It's all going to be on you.

Speaking of *The Exorcist*, if you're a devil in the office, you're going to find yourself exorcised.

---

## BUT BREAK: MEAN REVERSION

### "Dennis is smart and articulate, *but* he's got a nasty mean streak."

Mean reversion is a finance term that describes how over the long term markets return to their average or normal state. Congenital meanness is not normal, and it's a state you do not want to visit in the workplace. Meanness is a BUT of epic proportions. The symptoms of corporate meanness include but are not limited to the following:

- Embarrassing people in meetings.
- Making devastating personal comments about people who are not present to defend themselves.
- Belittling people for your own amusement. (What you think is funny is viewed by others as cruel.)
- Publicly expressing unwarranted disdain for members of senior management and/or the company.

- Sending out emails in which you "cut someone off at the knees" and include a long cc list—and perhaps an even longer bcc list.

If you are perceived as mean, everything you say and do thereafter will be seen through that lens. People will not follow you. They will fear you, but they will not follow you. If they know you are mean to others, they are rightfully concerned you will be mean to them someday, whether they are present for the attack or not. People will organize themselves quickly against someone they perceive as mean. They will look for allies. They will gather evidence. They will visit their human-resources representatives. They will visit with senior management to express their concerns and fears. They will go to great lengths to expel the mean manager before he or she comes after them. Survival is a powerful instinct, and a group of fearful people will mobilize their torches and pitchforks quickly if threatened by someone who is mean.

**SOLUTION:** We don't have any great advice on how to quickly overcome a deserved reputation for meanness. Nothing short of a complete mea culpa and a sincere effort to change your ways will work. The other thing you need is a lot of time. It can take years to repair the damage caused by acts of meanness. And while you are in the healing process, there is no margin for error. This requires you to stay right in the middle of the fairway with all of your interactions with colleagues. Don't crack jokes in meetings, because no one will think they are funny. Never poke fun at anyone, because it will be seen in the worst light. The wound left in the human psyche by meanness is immense. And every ill-conceived action or comment, however harmless, will pick at the scab on the wound. In this case, reverting to being mean even once guarantees the angry mob will come for you. The best advice we can give is preventative. Think before you say and do things. Make sure you never earn the mean label. Being mean is a BUT that is almost impossible to shake.

---

You have to exercise your BUT if you want to shrink it. You must look for and anticipate opportunities where you can work on the weakness you have become so painfully aware of. You must proactively seek out situations where you can show the world you are confronting your BUT and mastering it. If attention to detail is your weakness, the next report you write should be exquisitely detailed. If you are perceived as an arrogant know-it-all, look for an opportunity in a team meeting to say the most beautiful and humble words in the corporate dictionary, "I don't know." If you talk too much, then listen. If you listen too much, then talk. If you are marked as someone who is too detailed and has no vision, ask your manager for permission to create a report on what the business could look like ten years from now.

Whipping your BUT has three components to it:

1. Making a sincere effort to improve in the area where you are weak,
2. Reducing the negative impact your weakness has on the organization,

3. Changing how you are perceived by others so when they think of you they no longer think of your BUT, but rather your many strengths.

Whatever you need to do more or less of, just do it. That's the only way to whip your BUT into submission. In whipping your BUT, however, you don't have to go it alone.

## INVITE OTHERS TO WORK ON YOUR BUT

You will need help shrinking your BUT. And believe us, there are people around you who have a vested interest in seeing your BUT get smaller. They have been living with it for a long time. They are as motivated as you are, and even though it will mean they have to give up some good BUT gossip, they will help you. For some of your coworkers, this may be an unpleasant task, so beg and plead if you have to. It's that important. It's impossible for you to be vigilant about your BUT all of the time. We all get caught up in the demands and pressure of work, and we can periodically lose our self-awareness in the day-to-day chaos. You need your allies to be vigilant about your weaknesses. When they see them appear they have to stop you and point it out to you so that you can adjust.

Your sincere efforts to eradicate your BUT must be obvious to everyone. Make it impossible for anyone to surmise that your mission is inauthentic. We think everyone can agree that it's difficult to lead if your people do not believe you are genuine.

## BUT BREAK: INAUTHENTIC

**"Leah is dynamic and energetic,**
***but* people think she's a phony."**

If people think you are manipulative or phony, you have a BUT of biblical proportions. Most of us know a person in our office who speaks and acts with a specific personal agenda in mind. Every word is carefully chosen and situations are painstakingly managed to align with whatever self-serving motive they are pursuing. From their mouth comes an unending stream of self-promoting propaganda. The Inauthentic will tell the boss what he or she wants to hear and tell subordinates things that make Mr. or Mrs. Inauthentic look more important than they actually are. People who are inauthentic are not trusted. Their colleagues know their personal agenda is far more important to them than the company's agenda or the well-being of the colleagues around them.

**SOLUTION:** Being perceived as inauthentic is really tough to overcome. The first thing you have to do is decide if your goals and ambitions are the same as the company's. Then you have to decide if you are willing to partner with your colleagues to achieve a shared level of success. If you can do those two things, your career with the company is salvageable. You need to show people the success of the team is more important than your personal success. Your agenda must match the team's agenda. You must think before you speak. What am I saying? Why am I saying it? How will it be perceived by others? Am I saying these things for the advancement of the team or for my own self-promotion? Your team will know, so you had better know. You also need to build staff relationships on a deeper level. Have a barbecue at your house and invite the key folks you need to partner with to be successful. Get to know them personally, and allow them to see you as you are. Take an interest in them and find common ground and shared experiences. Go out for beers, for lunch, anything you can do in order to allow people to see your human side. People want a deeper relationship with their coworkers because they want to be able to trust them. Give them some good reasons to trust you. Get real, real fast.

---

To whip your BUT you must make a complete and honest commitment to fix the problem. Anything less than that will fail. And you will damage your credibility in the process. Ask your friends and allies to help you monitor and manage your BUT. Ask them, "Did I say I would commit to that initiative?" "Was I being stubborn and ignoring the objections of others?" "Did that comment come off as disingenuous?" Your friends and allies in the company will be more than willing to help you if you are committed to the cause. They can be your coaches and your cheerleaders. All you have to do is ask.

## COMPLEMENTING YOUR BUT

Notice that's "complementing" with an *e*, not an *i*. The last thing we want you to do is to go around the office saying nice things about your BUT—or anyone else's, for that matter. What we do want you to do is partner with people in your office who are very strong in the areas where you are weak. In fact you should surround yourself with them. Go find them. They are out there. When you spend time with them you will realize they, too, have weaknesses. And in many cases, their weaknesses may actually be your areas of strength. They say opposites attract. In the world of BUTs, that is certainly the case.

Let's look at two complementary BUTs side by side and see how their owners can work together to whip their BUTs in tandem.

---

## BUT BREAK: INDECISIVENESS

### "Kevin has integrity and passion, *but* he can't make a decision."

General George McClellan, leader of the Union forces during the Civil War, was paralyzed by indecisiveness. He had larger troop numbers and more resources than his Confederate foes, but he would not launch an attack into northern Virginia, where the enemy was assembling. He always wanted more information and time before taking action. Lincoln grew so frustrated with his lack of aggression he eventually relieved McClellan of his command.

Like generals, effective business leaders must be proactive; they must act in a timely fashion and with a sense of urgency. You will never have every bit of information, and there is no such thing as a perfect plan. You must aggressively engage a problem or a competitor in order to understand what you are up against. There is an old insightful boxing expression: "Every fighter has a plan until he gets punched in the face." He then must rely on his primal skills and instincts to defeat a competitor. In business, action produces information and information leads to the adjustments that help you achieve your objective.

**SOLUTION:** Don't wait until you have all of the information. Decide and act as soon as you have enough information. Trust your gut. Move forward and adjust as you get more information. If not, you too may be relieved of your command.

---

Find someone in your office who knows how to pull the trigger, and partner with them on your initiatives. If you're great at planning, bring them in to help you decide the right time to move.

---

## BUT BREAK: READY . . . FIRE . . . AIM!
### "Alexander is decisive and aggressive, *but* he acts before thinking things through."

Alexander Hamilton was the former Treasury secretary of the United States. He was killed in a gun duel by Aaron Burr, the sitting vice president. (It's pretty crazy if you think about it. Imagine Joe Biden and Timothy Geithner walking off twenty paces on the lawn outside the U.S. Capitol and then turning and firing at each other with 9mm Berettas.) Lore has it that Hamilton's brother-in-law gave him a gun with a hair trigger. This would allow Hamilton to fire the gun more quickly. Hamilton underestimated the sensitivity of the hair trigger and ended up firing the gun while it was still in the air. This provided Burr a free shot at Hamilton and he put a slug in his belly. Hamilton suffered greatly and died the next day. (Many historians say Hamilton purposely fired his gun into the tree above Burr believing Burr would do the same. If that's true, then we could write another segment on a BUT related to getting agreements in writing.)

**SOLUTION:** Pulling the trigger before thinking things through can be fatal to business careers. While speed is important, so is accuracy. Just ask Mr. Hamilton. Preparation is critical in things both big and small. Devise your plan. Be thorough. Make sure you have contingencies if things go off course. Be patient. Don't jump the gun. As legendary basketball coach John Wooden once said, "If you don't have time to do it right, how will you find time to do it over?"

---

To complement this BUT, look for someone notorious for meticulous planning, or maybe the person with indecisiveness as a BUT would be a great partner. Team up to find a happy medium between yourselves. She might temper your instincts to jump at the drop of a hat, and you might find yourself encouraging her to come out of her comfort zone. There's no better way to whip two BUTs at once than by partnering with someone who is the opposite of you.

Everyone's brain is programmed differently. Some people are great with numbers; other people are stronger with concepts. Some people see the smallest detail, where others can only see the big picture. Some people have terrific interpersonal skills, while others should be locked in a room with a computer, their contact with the outside world limited to the pizza-delivery guy. Some tasks are mastered easily because the person has a knack for it and they enjoy doing it. Other tasks are difficult and painful because they reside outside of the skill set, and an individual has no confidence they'll be able to do it. Having to do those difficult, out-of-the-comfort-zone tasks actually causes a physical reaction in our bodies. Our heart rate increases, our palms start to sweat, and the little voice in our head starts chanting, "You suck at this."

Over the years, we have learned how to complement our many BUTs that appear in the office. For example, Joe's strengths are dealing with and managing people, seeing market opportunities unfold, developing new investment products, and communicating and selling new concepts both internally and externally. Joe has many BUTs. He is disorganized. He has a short attention span. He is not detail-oriented. He is easily distracted. We could go on and on. The list is long, which is why Joe has surrounded himself with people who are good at what he stinks at.

For example, Joe is not good at mapping out the hundred steps and milestones in chronological order to go from concept to product. This is what is known as execution. Joe's friend and colleague Vijay says, "Vision without execution is hallucination."

Vijay is right. And if Joe did not have his management team members, Steve and Larry, he would be rolling around on the mats of a psych ward in a firmly fastened straitjacket. Steve and Larry are everything Joe is not. The tasks that make him nauseous make them smile. They think in a linear fashion. They are extremely organized and detail-oriented. Larry loves metrics and milestones and creates detailed work lists on every project they take on. Steve can see risks looming around corners and obstacles far down the road, and he devises solutions for all of them. Both of them follow up on every open item, and they make sure issues are resolved promptly. To some they can both be a pain in the butt. To Joe they are the perfect complements and antidotes to his many BUTs.

## SPEAK TO YOUR BUT LOUDLY AND OFTEN

You know what your BUT is. You have accepted it. And you are resilient and determined to shrink it. Now it's time to show the world your BUT. You need to launch your BUT-awareness campaign and let your colleagues know that you are working on it. Speak openly about the fact you have discovered it and that you are making a conscious effort and committing significant energy to shrink it. Acknowledging your weaknesses shows both enormous self-confidence and signifies a commitment to improvement.

Remember, your colleagues have been talking about your BUT for as long as you have worked with them. The coworkers who care about you will be relieved you are finally talking about it, too. The others, who want to step on your head as they climb the corporate ladder, are going to be disappointed to hear that your torn Achilles heel is being prepped for surgery. Have the confidence to announce your shortcomings and your commitment to improve. This puts your peers on notice that you are not going to be complacent about your BUT and they will be dealing with a much stronger competitor when the next big job opening comes along. Change how you are perceived by knowing how you are perceived.

---

## BUT BREAK: COMPLACENCY

**"Peter is well thought of by staff, *but* he's grown complacent over the years."**

When you are in the same job for a long time, you begin to get comfortable with how things work. The people, process, and culture have a familiar rhythm to them that can lull a manager and his staff into a state of complacency. World markets, industry competitors, and your customers are anything but complacent. If you are not experimenting, innovating, and responding to their ever-changing needs, you are on the road to oblivion. If you are a leader in an organization and you are not preparing for and adapting to a very different future, you'd better get moving or you'll be moved out. If this sounds like your personal BUT, you'd better find some aggressive staff members to push you toward the cutting edge and away from the cutting block.

**SOLUTION:** David Novak, the CEO of Yum! Brands, spoke

last year at Joe's company off-site event. He summed up the cure for complacency in what he referred to as the Hotshot Rule. He posed this question to the audience: "If the brightest and most capable young hotshot manager in your office were given your job today, what would be the first three changes he or she would make?" David then said, "Go and make those changes right now, so the hotshot manager doesn't take your job." Problems do not age well. Fix the things that are broken. Make the difficult decisions. Take the appropriate actions, or somebody else will while you're at outplacement services.

---

Whether you are viewed as indecisive or complacent, let your manager and your colleagues know you are aware of their perception and you are hell-bent on proving them wrong. Let people get to know the real you. Now go out there and take some risk. Build a robust project plan. Implement an innovative approach. Be bold with clients and ask for the business. And then ask again.

## GET YOUR BUT IN THE RIGHT SEAT

We have just reviewed why complementing your BUT is important, but making sure your BUT is a fit for certain roles is even more important. When one of Bob's colleagues is dealing with employee development issues, she always asks, "Is it an attitude or aptitude problem?" "Attitude" and "aptitude," two words that are only one letter apart, are at the root of many of the BUTs we are discussing.

Having the right attitude and aptitude for your specific role are the keys to business success. Do you generally enjoy what you are doing? Not every task. Not every day. But overall are you interested and engaged in the type of work you are doing? Does your job get you excited or at least give you some level of satisfaction? If your answer is yes, then your attitude at work should be pretty good. If your answer is no, then you are probably in the wrong field, which may be negatively impacting your attitude. We're quite certain that a bad attitude will negatively affect your performance and career.

---

## BUT BREAK: PASSIVE-AGGRESSIVE BEHAVIOR (PAB)

**"Marty talks tough in the cafeteria, *but* he's totally passive-aggressive."**

We call this BUT the granddaddy of them all. It's endemic and devastating. The workplace is the petri dish for passive-aggressive behavior and is absolutely the perfect environment for PABs to thrive and spread. Many people have some passive-aggressive tendencies, and more than just a few use it as their modus operandi. It's a coping mechanism and survival skill that has been honed by humans over the last few hundred thousand years.

When someone at work does not want to do something they have been told to do, they go to great lengths not to do it while never saying that they won't do it. This simply means the PAB will do everything he or she can to resist change without ever publicly protesting against the change. Why? Because PABs don't like confrontation, they avoid conflict, and they are afraid of being fired. So what do they do? They quietly resist. They complain. They show up late. They obstruct. They criticize. They procrastinate. They purposely forget to do things. They sulk. In the simplest terms they refuse to get on board and enact changes mandated by those in power. In his book, *Living with the Passive-Aggressive Man*, Scott Wetzler captures the essence of this affliction: "The passive-aggressive man may pretend to be sweet or compliant, but beneath his superficial demeanor lies a different core. He's angry, petty, envious, and selfish."

**SOLUTION:** Have you ever been passive-aggressive at work over some change you thought would negatively impact you? We bet you have. Anger, envy, pettiness, and selfishness are distinctive and annoying human traits. We all have displayed these at some point in our work life. It's okay to resist, as long as you do it quickly and quietly. Instead of sulking, why don't you go visit with the decision maker and get a better understanding of why the changes were made? If you listen to the reasoning behind the decision, perhaps it will be easier to accept it. Sooner or later you have to get on the bus or get run over by it. Why not be proactive and get on the bus sooner rather than later? You will probably get a better seat.

If you find that your passive-aggressive attitude has gotten worse over time, it could be a symptom of a pattern of managerial choices you disagree with but feel you have no power to counteract. If you have to go out of your way to connive and backstab to make your point (without making it look like you're making a point), then it might mean you're in the wrong place. The quickest way to cure PAB? Get out of there. Find a position where you don't have to be passive and where you don't have to be aggressive. You should be able to feel you can voice your point of view openly and effect change without resorting to dirty, behind-the-scenes tactics.

---

Are you naturally good at your job? Does it leverage your strengths? Do you feel strong and confident while you are at work? Or do you feel uncomfortable or vulnerable when performing critical tasks? If it's the former, you have the natural aptitude for your job. If it's the latter, you are either in the wrong role or you are in urgent need of training. Your natural skills may be poorly aligned with the job requirements, or you need more time in a classroom or with a mentor to get you up the learning curve.

A poor alignment of skills and job requirements will lead to a bad attitude or expose a low aptitude. It's much better if you assess and adjust this alignment long before your boss does.

## DOES THIS JOB MAKE MY BUT LOOK BIG?

When Joe was a freshman at Harvard University, an upperclassman gave him the most profound advice. He told Joe, "At Harvard you only have to be smart two days a year. Those are the days each semester you pick your classes." He was telling Joe not to take a course that would be beyond his intellect, not of interest to him, or one taught by a sadistic professor who likes to fail people. Do your research and homework on the course before you take the class. Unfortunately, Joe did not listen and he decided to try some pre-med courses in his first semester. The pre-med program has a "weeding out" process and Joe was a weed. In his second semester he was sent to the economics building, where most of his football teammates were.

The same is true at work. Only take a job that is aligned with your skills and interests. And never take a job that involves tasks you hate or things you are simply not very good at. If you feel awkward in social situations, don't go into the sales department. If math and numbers are not intuitive to you, don't give the finance or accounting group a try. Make sure you speak directly to people who work in the prospective group and have reported to that manager so that you understand the group's culture and what is required.

While different types of businesses have different expectations for timelines, meeting deadlines is always critical. If your workflow pace is naturally slow, don't choose a position that has quick, high-pressure turnaround times. The wrong job will make your BUT stand out.

---

## BUT BREAK: SPEED IS MEASURED IN TIME
### "Eugene is very thoughtful, *but* he's too damn slow."

In the NFL there is no substitute for speed. Joe had the opportunity to briefly play in the NFL back in the mid-1980s. He might have played longer if he could have run faster. Monte Kiffin, Joe's linebacker coach with the Buffalo Bills, said, "Azelby, you have the speed of a man twice your size." It took Joe a few days to realize it wasn't a compliment. In business, there is also no substitute for speed. If lack of speed is your BUT you could end up on the waiver wire like Joe.

Ask any CEO, what is your company's most important resource? Almost every CEO will say, "Our people." Isn't that nice? What an inspiring and original answer to an innocuous question. Unfortunately, it's complete BS. The most important resource of a company is *time*. People can be replaced. Time cannot be replaced. It's not renewable. You can't recycle it. It's precious and fleeting. That's it . . . full stop. No other resource is as important as time. What resource do people waste most often? You guessed it! Time! How is time wasted? Meetings with no clear purpose waste time. Long, rambling conference calls on which decisions are never made waste time. Business trips with unclear objectives waste time. Unprofitable customers waste the company's time. Ignoring deadlines and deliverables wastes time. Corporate bureaucracy is the greatest "time toilet" of all, as hours and hours of productivity are routinely flushed away by it. We'll let you in on a little secret: if your competitors are using their time more efficiently than you are, they will beat you every time.

**SOLUTION:** Act with urgency. Business is a race, and you have to run hard and fast. Short meetings with a purpose save time. Well-informed, quick decisions save time. Visiting key clients and understanding what they want saves time. Enforcing deadlines saves time. Cutting red tape saves time. If your manager or colleagues think you are too slow, pick up the pace. There is no substitute for speed. There is no more precious resource than time. Use it wisely and quickly.

---

A job that is not well aligned with your strengths is going to make your BUT look really big. A boss who does not value the skills you have and needs the skills you do not have will make your BUT look even bigger. Make sure you ask your Truth Teller, "Will this job make my BUT look big?" before you take it or even consider it.

While some people look to broaden their careers, others prefer a narrower path.

---

## BUT BREAK: GROUND-HOG DAY
### "Erik has incredible expertise, *but* I can't picture him doing anything else."

There is nothing wrong with being a focused expert. Some people take great pride in knowing more than anyone else in a specific area of knowledge or competence. They are the go-to expert in a very narrow subject. Some of these people also fear change and uncertainty. They have very small comfort zones and they try to stay inside of them. Recall the movie *Groundhog Day*, where Bill Murray's character wakes up day after day in Punxsutawney, Pennsylvania, and then relives the same day over and over again. For us, if we start a day knowing exactly what is going to happen, then we're not sure what the point is of living that day. This is what prison must be like. We don't want to be in prison. And Bill Murray didn't want to be in Punxsutawney. The same routine day in and day out is boring, and frankly, unnatural.

**SOLUTION:** If you are happy doing what you are doing, then focus all of your energy and expertise on making sure you remain the very best in that chosen field. You must be comfortable knowing that while you may be doing much of the same thing for the next ten to twenty years, there is enough depth and new development in the area to keep you interested and motivated for the long haul. Be mindful, of course, there could be major market disruptions or technology advances in your area of expertise that can potentially make you obsolete. If that happens, then you could have a real problem.

Also be aware that if you limit yourself to displaying a certain skill set, your coworkers may start to see you as capable in only those areas. You might be an excellent marketer, but unless you demonstrate that to your team, they might just think of you as a numbers person. Don't let your manager and peers pigeonhole your career, because what you're happy doing today might not be what you want to be doing tomorrow. Leave your options open, even if that means taking a risk and branching out from time to time.

---

While you can—and should be—searching for that perfect job that makes your BUTs look as small as possible, that's still no excuse for not working on eliminating those BUTs altogether. Ernest Hemingway said, "You can't get away from yourself by moving from one place to another." If you drag your BUTs from one job to another without ever addressing them, you'll find yourself constantly plagued by the same problems, no matter what the position or location.

## MOVING YOUR BUT FROM "A" TO "THE"

When you are pursuing a bigger and better job in your company, rest assured other qualified candidates are also competing for it. Yet human nature is such that we tend to only focus on ourselves. We'll confidently tell ourselves in our magic mirror, "I can do that job," and we go to our manager or the hiring manager and ask, "Do you think I am a candidate for that job?" More times than not the answer from the manager will be "Yes, I could see you in that role."

People love to hear they could be seen in that role; however, it is critically important that you understand how you are ranked against other competitors for that coveted job. Behind the reflective glass of your magic-mirror, there will be an army of talented internal and external candidates at your company's door trying to get their BUT in that same seat. If you have the experience, maturity, and general qualities to do the role, you will hear what you want to hear when you ask the hiring manager if it seems like a good fit. "Sure, you could do this job." That answer feels nice, but it's a meaningless throwaway validation for the manager to give.

The real question to ask is not "Am I *a* candidate for the role?" It is "Am I *the* candidate for the role?" It's an incredibly important distinction. The onus is on you to move the conversation and the hiring manager's perception of you from "a" to "the." How do your strengths compare to the other candidates'? How are your skills or experiences differentiated from others'? Most important, what is your reputation or brand within the firm? What do people say about you when you are not around? For an important job, the hiring manager is going to line everyone up and do a full scouting report on all the candidates. Make sure that your strengths are bigger and your BUTs are smaller than those of the other candidates before you waste a lot of time and energy chasing a job you never had a chance of getting.

As the economy remains stagnant and the unemployment rate remains high it's imperative that people continue to build and broaden their experience set to remain competitive. Unlike the earlier part of the decade, when companies were really concerned about retention, today many companies believe they can upgrade positions by looking outside their firm. In today's war for talent the corporations are in the driver's seat. The bigger your comfort zone, the bigger the job opportunity set.

---

### BUT BREAK: KING OF PAIN

**"Charles has mastered his job, *but* he refuses to leave or expand his comfort zone."**

The 1983 hit "King of Pain" by the Police should serve as a reminder to leave your comfort zone. Moving outside that zone involves risk, learning, changing, and sometimes pain and misery. Who wants that? Anyone who wants to get better, go further, and grow both personally and professionally should crave circumstances and assignments that are outside their comfort zone, and accept the possibility of failure. We will tell you the times when we grew the most professionally was when we were stretched to the limits of our skill, talent, and pain threshold. Those periods involve great misery when you are in them and great satisfaction once you've endured them.

**SOLUTION:** The expression "misery loves company" should be reversed. "Companies love misery" for their most promising managers, because it makes them stronger and better. Seek stretch assignments. Ask for new challenges. Do some things at work that make your palms sweat. Be the King or Queen of Pain!

---

# THE THEORY OF RELATIVITY

You don't have to be Einstein to understand that when it comes to career advancement, the theory of relativity applies. An employee's strengths and BUTs will be evaluated relative to anyone available who can do that job. People, however, like to view themselves in absolute terms: My name is Bill. I am intelligent. I am articulate. I am very experienced. I have a strong work ethic. I am effective and productive. I have been a loyal employee for fifteen years, and it's my time to move ahead. I should be promoted, because I have the résumé that is best suited for this job.

Bill's manager, however, views the world in relative terms with an eye to the future rather than the past: I am Bill's manager. Bill is all the things he says he is. That is why we hired Bill and why he has been successful here at our firm. He's an outstanding candidate for this big role that has become available. Bill's challenge is that Susan, who is currently in another unit, has a knowledge base that spans many of the critical issues facing our industry. Susan has a more relaxed presentation style that engages an audience, and she always nails the teaching moments. Like Bill, she is a tireless worker and a very dynamic and productive leader. Susan does not have as many years of experience as Bill in this particular sector, but she has more breadth and career upside. Could Bill do the job? Yes. However, promotions are not based on tenure, and our firm does not give out lifetime-achievement promotions. I am very confident Susan can do this job and also has the potential and skill set to do much bigger jobs. I am willing to take some risk with Susan's limited experience in the particular sector in exchange for that additional upside.

Notice that Bill did not get the promotion, even though there were no traditional BUTs that were holding him back. Bill, however, does have a BUT, and it looks like this: "Bill is highly qualified, *but* Susan is the better choice." That's the theory and practice of relativity at work.

# BE OPEN TO DIFFERENT ROLES

If you find yourself face-to-face with so many Susans that your career seems to have come to a screeching halt, you should be open-minded about your next steps. We have often seen people decline the offer to take on a new role and/or relocate to another division, perhaps in another city. Many times we've wondered if that individual fully appreciates the opportunity cost of turning down a new role. Throughout Bob's career, he accepted roles that he did not really want; nor did he believe he would learn anything particularly valuable by doing them. Boy, was he ever wrong! For example, he was a brand director at his large biopharmaceutical company, which is a highly coveted spot, when he was asked to lead a corporate-wide strategic initiative. He originally turned down the role but finally agreed because the organization wanted him to do it. He learned an unbelievable amount in this role and saw parts of his company he would have never been exposed to. The job also gave him great visibility because he was frequently meeting with senior VPs and executive VPs from a number of different divisions.

You think he would have learned from this. Of course not! He was then asked to move again to become the general manager of the firm's branch in the Netherlands. When our family heard about Bob's potential new position in Holland we all wondered how he would fare in the land of windmills, tulips, wooden shoes, and very tall people. (The last reference is the fact that the Dutch on average are the tallest people on earth, which provides the opening for a personal side story. Bob is about 5'10" tall. His brother and coauthor Joe is almost 6'2". Their house, growing up, had three very small bedrooms and a closet. That closet was Bob's bedroom. Bob asserts that if he had slept in one of the other bedrooms he would have been 6'3" and a Division I college basketball point guard. He claims that he suffered from "goldfish bowl syndrome" whereby he could only grow to a height constrained by the size of his environment. If you saw Bob's bedroom, you'd believe him.)

Okay, back to the Netherlands. Bob gave the job transfer some more thought and decided, "What the hell, let's do it." He packed up his four kids and pregnant wife and moved to a town just outside Eindhoven. In those two years in the Netherlands, he learned more about leadership both from a personal and professional perspective than ever before. Leading a business team that is culturally different was a challenge that required a significant adaptation of his management style. The first thing Bob learned is that the Dutch don't find him funny. And believe us, he thinks he's funny. He hit them with some of his best comic material and he could not generate a single smile. There he was laughing hysterically at his own jokes while the stoic (others would say intelligent) Dutch looked at him like he was an alien from another planet. Although the adjustment was hard, by immersing himself in a new culture, Bob never learned more in his life. He refers to his time in the Netherlands as the greatest life-learning experience he has had to date.

Here are just a few lessons learned in the Netherlands:

- Bob became comfortable delegating authority and relying on the local staff because they knew far more than he did.

- Although the Dutch culture is different from the American culture, both sets of employees want to work in a collaborative environment and be recognized for their contributions.

- Americans are more political and circumspect when communicating with management. The Dutch are very honest and direct. They will repeatedly tell you exactly what is wrong with the operation until you fix it.

- "Dutch Uncle" is the term used to describe a person who tells you not what you want to hear but what you need to hear. "Dutch Uncle" and "Truth Teller" are interchangeable terms.

- The Dutch are both kind and patient when training a new manager.

- If you trust your managers, listen to them, because in most cases they understand what experiences will help prepare you for a long and successful career.

**Wrap-up:** To get your BUT in the right seat, make sure that your talents and interests are well aligned with your key job functions. Don't take a job that will make your BUT look big. The right aptitude leads to the right attitude, and having both will lead to success. It's a competitive market out there, so make sure that your package of strengths and weaknesses compares favorably to those on the long list of candidates that also want the next big job. Be open-minded about your next role. It could be in an area of the company or a part of the world that you have never even considered. Don't get goldfish-bowl syndrome. You will only grow if you stretch yourself—so do just that.

# CHAPTER 4

# BUTS ABOUND

We've made it very clear so far that everybody has a BUT. So, needless to say, there are a whole bunch of BUTs in your office. Some BUTs relate directly to office culture, like working well with a team or dealing with a micromanaging boss. In this chapter, we'll discuss BUTs that come between you and your coworkers and have the potential of messing up your relationships and your career. If you haven't found your BUT yet, chances are it's going to come up soon.

## YOUR MANAGER AND YOUR BUT

A good manager should highlight your strengths and have a detailed discussion about your developmental areas in every annual review, if not more frequently. However, human nature is such that many people, including managers, have great difficulty addressing people's weaknesses or shortcomings. BUTs can be unpleasant to talk about because they hurt feelings and bruise egos. This is especially true when the owner is completely unaware of their BUT. It can be very embarrassing to learn that your large BUT has been a problem for an extended period of time.

A manager knows the emotional impact of confronting it head-on and more often than not will choose not to. Some managers will allude to a BUT and then only dance around the edges of it because they are too squeamish. Very few will throw it on the table and dissect it right in front of you. In fact, the bigger your BUT, the less likely it will get discussed. Small BUTs are more often identified, because managers believe that with some effort they can be fixed. Big, ugly BUTs are like the elephant in the room. Everyone can see it, but no one will talk about it.

Whatever your BUT may be, you need to help your manager or your Truth Teller give it to you straight. The best technique for doing that is providing your manager some distance and air cover between him or her and your BUT. Don't say, "Tell me what my weaknesses are." Instead ask this question: "When you are in meetings with senior management or my teammates, what do they say are my areas of weakness or development needs?" Since you have created the separation of third-party attribution for your manager, he or she is going to feel more comfortable giving you the truth you seek. Try this technique. It really works.

Here is an example of a small BUT that managers would be comfortable to speak with you about.

---

## BUT BREAK: SOONER RATHER THAN LATER
### "Katie is very detailed and thorough, *but* takes too long to deliver the final product."

Katie may be a perfectionist who will not deliver her work until it is thoroughly and flawlessly completed. That's great, but clients and markets don't wait for perfection. They need solutions, and they need them now. Sometimes "good enough today" wins out over "better tomorrow."

**SOLUTION:** Katie has a small BUT that can be easily corrected. The ingredients for success are all there. They just need to be properly modified. Katie can always provide fewer details in her report, or her manager can give Katie more lead time on a project. It's some combination of content and time management that can be adjusted to strike the right balance. A manager would be comfortable telling Katie how great her work is and suggest how she can be more efficient in her delivery of it. With time, experience, and coaching Katie will be able to find the right balance between content and time.

---

Another very manageable BUT involves how you communicate with your manager.

## BUT BREAK: BEAT YOUR BOSS
## TO THE PUNCH

### "Damien is a solid performer, *but* I always have to chase him down on the follow-up."

If you do not do this, we can guarantee you that your manager will let you know about it. When you have the opportunity to lead a very important project for your boss, make sure you update them before they ask you for an update. Most managers in today's working world are swamped with issues and struggle to stay updated on their important projects. In many cases the manager will be walking into work, exercising on a treadmill, or taking a shower, when all of a sudden, "What the hell is going on with Project X?" explodes into their mind. This causes the manager stress and anxiety, because they start to assume the project is off track. Without an update, the manager begins to wonder if the project manager is hiding something from them. It's human nature to fear the unknown and assume the worst.

What will intensely aggravate your manager is if you have not been keeping them apprised and they get asked about the project by *their* boss. Allowing your manager to be embarrassed by his or her superiors is a really bad outcome for you, too. In this unfortunate situation, even when you explain to the manager the project is on track, they will still be angry because you failed to protect them from being ambushed. The most successful people in an organization know how often their managers want to be updated, and they always make sure they beat that timeline by a few days or a few hours.

**SOLUTION:** Let's not overthink this one. Ask your boss how often they would like to be updated. Every boss is different, so why hazard a guess? You would be shocked by how many people never think to ask the obvious question. Give your boss updates a little more frequently than they requested. If you do it too often, they will let you know, and you can dial back the frequency. Most importantly, do a good job on the project. Frequent updates on poorly managed projects just get you fired sooner. When the project is moving ahead on schedule, communicate often, and your manager will love you and give you more projects. Even more importantly, inform your manager immediately if your project falls behind schedule and let him/her know you have a plan to address it.

Managers understand projects will hit bumps in the road. They just want to see them before they drive over them. The key message is that managers hate surprises. The more you ask on the front end and the more you communicate along the way, the less likely there will be any bad surprises on the back end.

Both of the previous BUTs are just the perfect size for a manager to deal with. Not only will confronting it directly benefit and protect them, but it will also make you a more efficient employee. You might not even feel the contact with this kind of BUT slap. It's the bigger BUTs, which don't have such cut-and-dried solutions, that are more difficult for a manager to broach—and they result in a BUT slap that stings a lot more.

Managers can live with mistakes as long as they are acknowledged by those who made them. If you can't admit a mistake, that's a different story. Managers have too much to do to be bothered with the blame game.

---

## BUT BREAK: IT WASN'T ME

### "Alice is diligent and efficient, *but* she will never admit to making a mistake."

Can you imagine living a life in which you are deathly afraid of admitting to a mistake you made? Or can you picture if your brain were wired in such a way that it would be incomprehensible that you could ever make a mistake? Or can you envision knowing that you made the mistake but that your personal policy is to never admit to anything?

This scenario reminds us of the song "It Wasn't Me," by the rap artist Shaggy. In the song, Shaggy's girlfriend walks into his apartment and finds him in a compromising position with another woman. If fact, she is in the apartment so long that she finds him in multiple compromising positions. As per the lyrics, Shaggy's defense strategy is to repeatedly tell his girlfriend, "It wasn't me," no matter what she saw him do.

Leadership is about taking responsibility for mistakes or bad outcomes. When some maniac was putting cyanide in Tylenol capsules, Johnson & Johnson took immediate responsibility for their customers' safety and got it off the stores' shelves as quickly as possible. Those actions saved the brand. Contrast that with Toyota, which denied and argued for weeks that their gas pedals were not sticking. The CEO finally took responsibility and later apologized to the American public, but the brand damage and the consumer mistrust were significant.

There are people who simply will not own up to mistakes, and they can be really difficult to deal with. Their great imperfection is not their mistakes, but rather their inability to see or admit they screwed up. No matter how clear the error and where the fault lies, the "Wasn't-Mes" of this world will create an elaborate self-reasoning loop that ends with denial or the mistake being someone else's fault. If you manage a "Wasn't-Me" employee, you're probably bald from pulling your hair out every time this happens. "It wasn't me" may not be a fatal BUT, but it's unbelievably annoying, and it undermines the offender's integrity and personal brand.

**SOLUTION:** We all make mistakes. Stuff happens. If you can't admit to making a mistake, we would like to invite you to join the human race with all of its imperfections. Come make mistakes with the rest of us, and perhaps learn from them along the way. If an elaborate apology for making a mistake is beyond your reach, try this little expression to let the world know you are like the rest of us: "My bad." Those two simple words are unbelievably effective on the basketball court or in the office.

"My bad" is an efficient proclamation of your humanity and your imperfection. Use it often. You won't be celebrated for your mistake, but you'll be applauded for your maturity.

---

We've talked quite a bit about how perception is reality. Your manager's perception of you and your performance should really be viewed as the center of your career universe. Being proactive with your manager and admitting to mistakes are a great way to improve your boss's perception of you. Above all, avoid anything that makes you annoying to your higher-ups. Here is a BUT that is very manageable but really tries the patience of your manager.

---

## BUT BREAK: PREMATURE SELF-ADULATION (PSA)
**"Tommy keeps asking for a promotion, *but* he hasn't mastered the job he has."**

This is a very common BUT among super-ambitious young professionals, especially those who have graduated from top-notch business schools and have a lot of student loans to pay off. Many of them visit their manager and talk about their next opportunity and challenge—and the higher levels of compensation that will go along with it. Those afflicted with PSA are both impatient and overly confident.

When approached by someone with PSA, the question we

always ask is "Have you nailed the job you already have?" They often look at us in the same way a dog watches television. Their head tilts, and they hear the words, but they don't really comprehend what we are saying.

After a prolonged pause, the most common response we get is "I think so."

"You think so?" we say. Face it, no good manager is going to give you a bigger job until you have crushed the job you currently have. Players batting .235 in AAA baseball do not get called up to the major leagues. Players who are batting .350 do. In the business world you had better be batting over .900 if you are going to push for a promotion.

**SOLUTION:** You should be doing your current job better than anyone who has ever done it before. You have to master every aspect of that job. The job you want to leave behind should be bigger, broader, and more complex than the job you were first given. Until you have done all that, do not ask your manager or anyone else in the organization about your want or need for career advancement or a big pay raise. Asking for a larger role too soon is like spiking the football on the two-yard line. You will look ridiculous. First, nail the job you have. Do that, and good things will happen. Here is some great advice once received in a fortune cookie: "Unbridled ambition is like a bad rash. It's best to keep it covered."

---

Now let's get to some meaty BUTs that no manager wants to touch. It takes a hardened Truth Teller to bring these BUTs to the forefront. The best way to handle these BUTs is to identify them in yourself before your manager is forced to take care of them. The longer these BUTs fester, the closer you are to getting popped.

## BUT BREAK: ARROGANCE DEFINED
**"Alec is really talented, *but* he's so arrogant."**

Arrogance: an attitude of superiority manifested in an overbearing manner or in presumptuous claims or assumptions. Wow, this is one of the most difficult BUTs to get out from under. When colleagues describe someone as arrogant, they are saying they don't like or trust that person. "Arrogant" is a catch-all label that is devastating to the employee it is bestowed upon. How does one stop being arrogant? How does a manager coach someone not to be arrogant? What manager has the time, energy, or patience to teach someone how to be endearing, how to be liked, how to be trusted? Not many, and that's why being perceived as arrogant is so damaging and so difficult to overcome.

We chose the name Alec because there is someone with this name you know that at least in our minds has recently transformed his persona from "always arrogant" to "episodically likeable." To us, Alec Baldwin of *The Hunt for Red October* and *Glengarry Glen Ross* fame was an arrogant, conceited, narcissistic, self-righteous, outspoken, and talented movie star. Today he is a hilarious, offbeat, and self-deprecating TV star and pitchman. How did this public-persona transformation happen? Alec

Baldwin simply unveiled other parts of his personality, including humor and humility. He made us laugh on *30 Rock* and he seems to laugh at himself in his wacky commercials. He revealed a quality in himself people can really appreciate . . . a good sense of humor. By doing so, Alec became more like all of us. To some, he may still be a self-centered jerk, but he's a more likable jerk now.

**SOLUTION:** If you have an extremely courageous manager who has told you that you are perceived as arrogant, you have a big mountain to climb and a lot of work to do. First, you must accept your colleagues probably don't like you and they certainly don't trust you. That is very painful to hear, difficult to reconcile, and even harder to fix. But if you are told you are arrogant, that is the reality you must deal with. You are doing things and saying things that people don't like. Or you are cold and aloof and people fear you and your indifference. Worst of all, you give everyone around you the impression that you think you are better than they are.

How do you correct this? How does someone become liked and trusted? It's not easy. You must go back and find out what you did and who you did it to that was perceived so negatively. Apologize for what was done, and never do it again. It sounds too simple, but very few people do this. Next, you must figure out a way to allow people to get to know the real you. You must become more like the people around you so they can identify with you. Show them pictures of your family. Talk about your spouse and children. Discuss with them the challenges of parenthood or caring for an aging parent. Share with them your hobbies, your passions, and even your fears. Most importantly, take an interest in *their* lives. Ask them questions about things that are important to them. Let them waste a few company minutes sharing with you their challenges, fears, and passions. It will be time well spent. There is no playbook for removing the arrogance BUT. However, if you are opening up to people and encouraging them to open up to you, we guarantee they will like you and trust you a little more than they did before.

---

No matter what the situation, whether you're trying to hide a mistake or paint a rosy picture for your manager, there is no excuse for lying. Be honest with yourself and your coworkers.

---

## BUT BREAK: LYIN' EYES
### "Neil appears earnest, *but* he has difficulty telling the straight truth."

The 1975 hit, "Lyin' Eyes" by the Eagles illuminates the dangers of not being truthful.

We are proud to say we have not seen many incidents of outright lying in our careers, but we have both seen people misremember or spin things. An individual can have recollections of what was said or what was decided that are dramatically different from those of other people in the room. We have seen people be so emphatic about what they or someone said, even when it's contradicted by the other twenty people in the room. Sometimes we only hear what we want to hear. That's human nature.

We have also seen people spin the truth or the data in order to strengthen their position or move their agenda forward. They will omit information that weakens their position or selectively add data or facts that support their position. They will do so even when they know the information is neither relevant nor applicable to the issue under discussion. While we can argue the differences between misremembering, spinning, manipulating, misusing, or omitting data, the fact remains that anything less than 100 percent disclosure and truthfulness is bad for you and your company.

**SOLUTION:** As an employee, you have an obligation to provide your management and your colleagues the truth, the whole truth, and nothing but the truth, so help you God. Truth is the foundation of integrity. When we were growing up our father would say, "Always tell the truth, because it's the easiest thing to remember and the right thing to do." There ain't no way to hide your lyin' eyes, so put all the cold, hard facts on the table for everyone to see.

---

Finally, here's a BUT that your boss might not even realize is a problem. In fact, your boss might *like* this BUT of yours because it makes him or her feel like they're constantly doing a great job. But if you keep this up, you're going to make yourself redundant. It's okay to argue with your boss.

## BUT BREAK: YES-MAN
### "Paul has a big title, *but* he's just a yes-man."

This 2008 film *Yes Man*, starring Jim Carrey, is about a man who tries to improve his life by saying "yes" to everything. Sounds like a funny premise for a movie, but it's a complete flop as a career strategy. Yes-men are blindly obedient stooges who agree with everything their boss says and does. What a boss should really want and needs is a "Dr. No." That is, a person who will disagree with the boss when the team is about to make a poor decision. We should all have people around us who have a different view or unique perspective. We want people to tell us, "That's a really stupid idea, and here's why," or someone who says, "That's an interesting strategy, but this one is better," or someone who says, "Are you out of your mind?" whenever they hear one of our bad ideas.

**SOLUTION:** Form your own views, and communicate them confidently. Argue the other side of issues, and challenge your boss's assumptions. This will make both of you better and stronger. If you always agree with your boss, one of you is not needed. Who do you think that is?

We all want to be perfect, and we expect the same from our managers. Unfortunately, every one of us is far too human, and we don't always deliver what others need from us. Managing people is a very difficult job, and giving reports the honest feedback they need is a tall order. If you take too long to deliver projects, you'll probably hear about it. If your manager wants more frequent updates, you'll know it. On the other hand, if you can't admit mistakes, your manager may not have enough evidence or guts to openly question your integrity, even though he or she will have doubts about your honesty. A manager may not want to burst your premature self-adulation bubble, for fear of ruining your confidence. And very few managers want to tell you that you are arrogant, because they have no idea how to help you overcome it. It's easy to teach people what to do, but it's very hard to teach people how to be. Therefore, the bigger and more challenging your BUT, the less likely your manager will confront you with it.

## YOUR TEAM AND YOUR BUT

Some jobs require you to interact with your team members more than others. And different jobs also require different types of interactions. Some office environments champion email conversation powered by shared documents, while other office cultures prefer the comfort of a conference room. All of these types of interactions give opportunities for new and different BUTs to develop. Make sure that when you're working with a team, you don't fall victim to one of these weaknesses. Small as they may be, they're sure to be the first ones that your coworkers notice.

## BUT BREAK: THE ABYSS
### "Albert has the information, *but* he won't respond to my calls or emails."

*The Abyss* is an underwater sci-fi movie directed by James Cameron of *Titanic* fame. (He clearly has a water fetish.) A team of Navy SEALs goes diving for a lost nuclear submarine miles under the ocean surface and makes contact with alien underwater creatures. "Abyss" is defined as an "immeasurable chasm or void of space and time." We use it to describe the person at the company who never returns phone calls or responds to emails. Messages go into the cold dark Abyss, but they don't come out. A deadline is looming. Their input is either wanted or needed. After numerous attempts, hours, days, or weeks pass with dead silence. The "Abyss" in your office may not be an alien, but his or her radio silence will alienate everyone.

**SOLUTION:** Unless you have died or been admitted into the federal witness protection program, you must respond to your colleagues. If an answer or acknowledgment is needed, do it as soon as you read the email or listen to the voice mail. There is no time like the present, because it's hard to forget things in the present. If the response requires some thought, just write, "Got it, I'll be back to you ASAP." Put a note on your calendar if you are prone to forgetting these types of commitments. Studies have shown the more senior the person is in a company, the quicker the response time. Maybe that's why they got to their lofty position.

While it seems that nowadays you can go a whole day interacting with people solely via a screen of some sort, there will always be times when you are required to attend meetings with your coworkers face-to-face. And though, at first, the time away from your office or cubicle seems like a breath of fresh air, some meetings can start to feel just as stifling. If you find yourself zoning out in these settings, listen up. This next BUT might be yours.

## BUT BREAK: THE BORED OF DIRECTORS

**"Joe shows up for the management meetings, *but* he does not consistently engage like his peers."**

Another BUT of Joe's has to do with business meetings. He doesn't like meetings, especially meetings where there are many people in the room and decisions are neither planned nor actually made. We're talking about those informational presentations where the materials are sent to the participants beforehand, and then the presenter takes us through it page by page.

These meetings make Joe really bored and tired. We're talking *crazy* tired. They drain his energy and leave him feeling like a bear hit with a tranquilizer dart. He feels the same way after playing golf (not his game) or going shopping at the mall against his will. By the end of the meeting, he's exhausted and cranky, even though he did not do very much. During these meetings he thinks about all the things he needs to do and will often take out his BlackBerry and just start doing them. It's quite rude to the speaker, but sometimes he can't help himself.

Meetings with more than ten people around the conference table are his kryptonite. If he is not responsible for something or doesn't have the intimate knowledge to opine on or change it, he's just not that interested. (Sorry, but it's true.) He sits quietly in meetings thinking about the things he does know, can control, or act upon. His colleagues, however, seem to be much more engaged. They ask questions and make comments on the issues and materials, even if those things are outside their area of responsibility or expertise. Joe wishes he had the interest and discipline to do that. But he seemingly doesn't, and perhaps it's a BUT that is limiting his contributions and even his advancement.

**SOLUTION:** Now that we have provided pathetic reasons and lame excuses for Joe's disengagement that make him feel better about himself, he needs to fix this problem. If the company is paying Joe to be in a meeting, he'd better make damn sure that he contributes to that meeting. If he is not an expert on the topic, he can certainly facilitate the meeting by getting the attendees focused on the purpose. He should be asking important questions, such as "Did everyone read the material?" "Are there questions on the material?" "Should we go right to questions?" "Are we here to make a decision, or is the presentation just informational?" "What does the presenter need from this committee?" These types of questions will help make the meetings shorter, more focused, and more likely to lead to a decision or action. And Joe probably won't be nearly as bored and tired if he is engaged.

Working with a team means you have to be a team player. Teammates don't necessarily always have to agree, but it's unacceptable to go behind your team's back when you don't agree with a decision.

---

## BUT BREAK: THE HALLWAY HERO
### "In meetings Frank seemingly supports decisions, *but* then he complains about them afterward."

We can't help but think of the refrain from Foreigner's hit song "Juke Box Hero" when we use this Hallway Hero term.

It's decision time. The management team has met and decided to go forward with the multimillion-dollar marketing program that will allow the company to leapfrog its competitors and wrest away profitable market share. It was a three-hour meeting, in which all of the risks and opportunities were fully vetted. A vote was taken at the conclusion of the meeting, and there was unanimous support to move forward. The marketing team was congratulated for their thorough and thoughtful presentation, and everyone was excited to start working toward the launch.

Then Frank, a member of the management team, tells his staffer in the hallway the program will never work and the company is pissing away millions of dollars. In the meeting Frank said nothing. He actually raised his hand in support of the project. Then he went out of the room and trashed the decision in front of a colleague. That's what a Hallway Hero does.

This is one ugly, two-faced BUT. If you have ever done this, you need to understand how destructive this behavior is to your company. If your boss finds out about your behavior, he or she should fire you. And you will deserve to be fired. An employee who subversively undermines the decisions and initiatives of his or her own company might as well be working for the competition. In fact, he or she is far more dangerous than any competitor, because the employee has access to information and can influence the views and attitudes of others in the firm. The corrosive impact this type of person can have on strategy and morale is frightening.

**SOLUTION:** If this is your BUT, get rid of it right now. If you have a dissenting view, let your colleagues know about it. Perhaps your view is the correct one, but it's of no value if you do not share it. Maybe you could save the company from an expensive ill-fated marketing program. Frank's behavior increases the chance his company will have an expensive marketing mistake.

Companies need heroes in conference rooms where big issues are discussed and difficult decisions are made. They don't need cowards skulking around the hallways trashing decisions and destroying team morale. If you share your dissenting view and the company still wants to proceed with the recommendation, try a second time to dissuade them. If you are overruled a second time, you need to accept the decision and get on the bus. Your responsibility now is to do everything in your power to help the program be successful. That's what corporate leaders do. Don't be a Hallway Hero.

We titled this section "Your Team and Your BUT," because unless you're in a department of one, you work with a group of peers. While the walls of your cubicle or door to your office can seem like the impenetrable barrier between your work-space and the outside world, there are people on the other side whom you have to get to know if you want to move ahead. Here's a BUT that needs a little more exposure.

---

## BUT BREAK: INVISIBLE INK
**"The interactions I've had with Eileen have been positive, *but* nobody really seems to know her."**

Long-timers often tell young professionals if they put their heads down and work hard, good things will happen. That may have been the case twenty-five years ago, but today the busi-ness world is too complex, the hierarchy too flat, and work pro-cesses too collaborative for that old-fashioned career strategy. In today's environment you have to be visible, because invis-ible people get overlooked. It's imperative that you get to know people and they get to know you.

**SOLUTION:** Speak up in meetings. Sit at the table and not in a chair along the wall. Ask a good question or add an important point. That's the quickest and best way to be noticed. People leaving the meeting will say, "Who was that woman asking the questions?" Volunteer for special projects. Get involved in the corporate community outreach programs. Step up to organize the holiday party. Networking is not only incredibly valuable to shaping a career; it's fun and rewarding. The most effective way to network is to befriend your company's best networkers. Every company has people who know more people and are known by more people. They are the connectors of the company who fly around the organization, like bees in a field of wildflowers, cross-pollinating information and friendships. These people are easy to identify. They are positive, energetic, and disarming. They take interest in others and are never too busy for a friendly interaction with a colleague. Become their friend, and you'll make many friends. Connecting with connectors is a winning strategy to gain visibility.

On the project and tasks front, too, you also need visibility. Your colleagues have to know and understand what you are working on or they may assume you are not working. How many times have you heard people in your office say, "I have no idea what he or she does"? It is said in such a way that whatever that person is doing cannot be very valuable. To avoid being the subject of that comment, let people know what you are doing.

In addition to communicating your contributions you should also look for projects that will give you the opportunity to work with senior executives or with people outside your immediate group. If the project involves a presentation, work hard to position yourself for a speaking part and a seat at the table. Show the world all that you have to offer. And never assume that someone else is doing that for you.

On the opposite side of the spectrum, being too focused on yourself has equally negative consequences. This next BUT reminds us of Audrey, the man-eating plant in *Little Shop of Horrors*. If you feed this BUT, it will grow so large that it will swallow up everyone in the office.

---

## BUT BREAK: THE EGOMANIAC

**"Seymour is smart and talented, *but* he's got a huge ego."**

When we were growing up in Dumont, New Jersey, a junior football coach of Joe's used to say, "Gentlemen, you must swallow your pride if you want to shit humility. And we will shit humility." What he was telling our young, formative selves in his own unique way was that championship teams have no room for individual egos or arrogance. His philosophy was simple. The team is always more important than the individual. Coaches, players, and parents must respect each other. That same respect will be shown to opposing teams, referees, and anyone else who comes in contact with our football program. We take the field in a humble fashion, and we leave the field humbly, regardless of the outcome. Showboating, taunting, and/or excessive celebration are banned. In fact any celebration is banned. He would always say, "When you score a touchdown, just hand the ball to the referee, and look like you have been there before."

Some people view themselves as so important they consider their arrogance and bad behavior the price others have to pay to keep their talent in the firm. They view themselves as so valuable that the rules of society and the company do not apply to them. They are the show. They are "it," and everyone should know it. They truly believe the firm would collapse the day they did not show up for work. They make up their own rules. They don't show up for meetings. They don't return phone calls. They don't support corporate initiatives. They are disrespectful of senior management and show disdain for the company. They can be belligerent and disrespectful to others. If you tell an egomaniac there is no "I" in TEAM, they'll turn around and tell you that there is a "ME" in TEAM.

**SOLUTION:** If egocentric behavior is your BUT we urge you to start your own company so you can create a culture that can accommodate your massive ego. If you want to stay with your current employer, you must take a step outside yourself and see the bigger picture. The firm is larger than you. You're not doing anybody any favors by showing up to work every day. The company can and will succeed without you. Your self-centered attitude is certainly not garnering you any respect or credibility with your colleagues. The best way to repair the damage you've already done is to turn around and acknowledge the contribution of your teammates. Each time you have a success, make it a team success and congratulate everyone who contributed to it. You are only as good as the people around you. If you are successful I suspect that they're pretty good, too. Let them know it.

If you are the egomaniac's boss, it's time for you to step up and represent the interest of the company. Your people are watching the egomaniac closely, and they are watching your reaction and response to the situation even more closely. In the eyes of your employees, an egomaniac is the equivalent of an opposing baseball pitcher who keeps "plunking" them at the plate. As the leader of the group you are your team's pitcher, and you have the obligation to protect your people. That means throwing a high fastball at the head of the egomaniac. That's right! You have to fire the ball right at the egomaniac to show that you are the boss and their behavior will not be tolerated. And when you do this, there will be one of two responses. The egomaniac will charge the mound and be fired. Or the egomaniac will get up off the ground with a welt on their head with a renewed respect for you and the people you represent. Remember, a good team will almost always beat a good player. And big egos destroy teams. The humble teams we played for in our youth quietly won a lot of championships.

## YOUR REPORTS AND YOUR BUT

If you manage a team, your reports are painfully aware of your BUT. That's because it's negatively impacting them in some shape or form. Your BUT is likely a source of stress, inconvenience, annoyance, and extra work for them. If your colleagues like you they will be more accepting of your BUT, and they will try to cover it when you expose it to people outside of your immediate group. If they don't like you, they are waiting for the day when senior management will see your BUT for what it is and take action against it. If they *hate* you, they will make every effort to show everyone, especially your boss, how big your BUT is so they get a new boss as soon as possible. We can almost guarantee you there is something you are doing today that is bugging the hell out of the people around you. Read on to discover those BUTs that are least desirable when managing a team.

If you have this next BUT, we will guarantee you that your colleagues will have little tolerance for any of your other BUTs.

---

## BUT BREAK: THE MICROMANAGER
### "Michelle is dedicated, *but* she micromanages everything."

Almost everyone has had an experience with a micromanager. And no one has ever had a good experience. They give you an assignment and a future delivery date, and then they check in hourly for updates and assurances. Then they carpet-bomb you with questions. "Is there a first draft I can read?" "Have you thought about this?" "Have you called this person or that person?" "Why are you doing it this way?" "Did you forget about this or that?" "May I make a suggestion?" You just want to scream at the micromanager, "Get out of my face, and let me do the job you are paying me to do!" We're not recommending you scream at your micromanager, but we would understand if you did.

The micromanagers are simply the corporate version of "helicopter parents." You know the parents we're talking about. They have weekly parent-teacher meetings if little Jimmy isn't getting straight A's. They call some other kid's parents because that kid said something mean to their little Jimmy. They walk on to the T-ball field to complain to the coach that Jimmy only got up to bat twice when some of the other kids got up three times.

The outcomes are generally the same for the micromanagers and helicopter parents. The first result is that the employees and children never learn to think and fend for themselves, which impedes every aspect of their professional or personal development. The second common outcome is the employees and children will resent the micromanager or helicopter parents. The kids will rebel by using drugs, alcohol, or dating someone they know their parents will hate. And when they come of age, they will choose a university far away from the heavy hands of their overbearing parents. Employees are no different. They too will rebel against a micromanager. But instead of ill-advised piercings, they will look to transfer internally or jump at the first job offer from another company.

**SOLUTION:** If you are a micromanager, talented people will not work for you. And if you don't have talent on your team, you will fail as a manager. It's that simple. Think about why you need to control everything. What triggers that need? Did someone let you down? Did someone disappoint you? Why don't you trust your reports to do their jobs? Get over it so you can give your people some breathing room to develop their talents. Let them experiment. Allow them to make some mistakes they can learn from and grow stronger. Let them earn their pay. Allow them to "cut and scar" the way we did as kids and young professionals on our way up the ladder of life.

Micromanaging is also unbelievably inefficient. Every second you spend overlooking the work of your subordinates, you are not doing the work your boss expects from you. Remember, it's much easier to climb a ladder when you are looking up rather than looking down.

---

As a manager your job is to lead, coach, and motivate your staff. If you have an underperforming staff member, it's your job to either improve their performance or manage them out. At all costs, you need to protect your peers from having to deal with your underperforming staff members in the future.

---

## BUT BREAK: THE FRED SANFORD
### "Fred manages a top-notch team, *but* he passes off less desirable employees to other departments instead of dealing with them himself."

Fred Sanford, of the old TV comedy *Sanford and Son*, ran a junk-yard and was a creative salesman. He used all kinds of stories and tactics to sell his junk to unwary buyers.

A corporate Fred Sanford is someone who gives good reviews to poorly performing employees in order to help them transfer to other departments. A Fred Sanford lacks the courage to manage or dismiss problem employees, so he or she facilitates their move to other departments. Accepting a Fred Sanford's former team members is the equivalent of waking up one day and find-ing your neighbors' junk strewn around your living room.

**SOLUTION:** Don't pawn off poor performers on your col-leagues. It's your job to manage up their performance or manage them out the door.

---

How you interact with your team and how they receive you are vitally important. Everyone has BUTs, and you do, too. How the team feels about you as a person and as a contribu-tor will determine how tolerant they are of your weaknesses. Will they help you cover your BUTs, or will they work hard to expose them? If they respect you they'll shrug off your mi-cromanaging as being detailed. If you are condescending but they think you are a good person, they'll say, "He can be a jerk, but he's our jerk." If they don't like you, then you are vulner-able, and they will come after you with a vengeance once you are weakened. Know where you stand with the people around you. And commit to improving your relationship with them by fixing the things you do that make their jobs harder. Put simply, be nice to people and they will support you. Treat them badly, and what goes around comes around.

## EMBRACE YOUR BOSS'S BUT

We were going to write, "Kiss Your Boss's BUT," but if you are smart, you are already doing that. Like you, your boss has a BUT, or in some cases, multiple BUTs. They can be large. It's your job to cover them. You must spend time observing, analyzing, and understanding your boss's BUTs and determine which are the largest and most visible. It's critically important that you understand where your boss is weak and vulnerable and position and align your skills to complement those areas. If your strengths protect and cover your boss's BUTs, you are absolutely golden. Think of the power and job security that goes along with being the person standing ready to provide what is missing in your boss's toolbox. Making your boss and his or her BUT look good leads to more responsibility and advancement.

One goal you should have is to establish yourself as your manager's left tackle.

---

## BUT BREAK: THE BLIND SIDE
### "Jill is a strong leader, *but* she has a blind spot with one of her direct reports."

This heartwarming movie is based on the true story of a homeless, over-sized, African American boy who gets taken in by a white family and discovers his unique talents in the game of football. It's called *The Blind Side* because the young man plays the left-tackle position. This is the most important position on the offensive line, because it protects a right-armed quarterback from the oncoming pass rusher attacking from his blind side.

Chances are your manager also has a blind side, in that he or she may not be able to see everything that's going on in the group from their vantage point. Risks may be developing in the business your manager cannot see. There may be someone on the team who is underperforming or damaging the group's culture, which your boss may be unaware of. This gets even more challenging if the employee in question is good at managing up or has a strong personal or professional relationship with the boss.

Some years ago, Joe had a large blind spot with a member of his management team. From Joe's seat, he could only see the good work this person was doing delivering the things Joe needed. He could not see that this individual was damaging the esprit de corps of the team below. It took an intervention by the courageous members of Joe's management team to shine the bright light on this situation and make him aware of the problem. They gathered as a group in Joe's office. They sat him down and told him exactly what was going on with this person and the negative impact it was having on them. It was hard to hear. Joe was astounded and embarrassed that he had such a large blind spot. The damage to the team was severe enough that Joe had to ask the problem person to leave. It was very difficult for Joe, because he had a very good working relationship and personal friendship with the offender. Joe did what was needed to be done, thanks to the courageous colleagues who forced him to confront a problem unknown to him at the time. They were all his left tackles protecting his blind side.

**SOLUTION:** If blind spots are one of your manager's BUTs, you need to be their left tackle and protect them. You need to have the courage to be the Truth Teller with these types of unpleasant situations. It's your job to support your manager by giving them the information they need to improve the business and protect themselves and the team for which they are responsible. No matter how difficult the conversation or the intervention will be, it's your duty to initiate it.

---

Another good career-advancement idea is to do the unpleasant heavy lifting when your boss has a weak backbone.

---

## BUT BREAK: MR. SOFTEE
### "Bill has the intellect for the job, *but* he's just too soft."

When we were kids this was the name of the ice-cream truck company that cruised through our neighborhood. They had the best chocolate and vanilla soft ice-cream swirl. The truck would blare its unmistakable melody throughout the neighborhood, usually when our mom was putting dinner on the table. We would yell and plead to get ice cream, and our mother would have to stand her ground and say no, to our great disappointment. Our mom was an absolute saint, but we're sure she hated that Mr. Softee guy and his musical truck.

Managers can also be a Mr. or Ms. Softee. They can be too nice and too ambiguous when they need to be tough and exquisitely clear. Some managers don't know how to firmly say "no." They allow employees to start pet projects that have little chance of success and drain the firm's resources. In the Darwinian world of corporate politics, being a Mr. Softee can hinder team performance and delay difficult decisions. There are some other practical risks of being too soft. People can take advantage of a good-natured manager. They may try to manipulate him or her. In extreme cases, a Mr. or Ms. Softee can be bulldozed or intimidated by an aggressive subordinate. Think how is easy it would have been for my mom to say yes to the ice-cream pleas of her four children. She never did. The ice cream would ruin our appetites, and the expense was not a good use of our family's limited financial resources. Mom was no Mrs. Softee. She knew how to say no, and we were far better off because of it.

**SOLUTION:** If your manager is a Mr. Softee, it's your job to toughen him up. Point out to him how and why he is being exploited or manipulated. Help him get to the tough decision or confront a difficult employee. Keep the boss focused on the facts. Don't allow him or her to introduce distractions that delay the tough business decisions your group faces. Embolden him to take decisive action, however challenging or uncomfortable the situation. A manager with a Mr. Softee BUT needs a "hard-ass" ally on his team.

---

## BUT BREAK: HELP ME HELP YOU
### "Margaret is extremely capable,
### *but* she refuses to delegate to others."

If you work for someone who can't delegate, "Help me help you" should be a constant refrain when speaking with your boss. Some managers cannot let go of tasks and responsibilities, even though they need to if they want to move up. Perhaps they feel more secure in their job when they control all tasks. They may want to feel indispensable so they don't let go of work. Maybe they have difficulty directing others, so they just do it themselves. Whatever it is, you have to get your boss to delegate more to you so that you can grow and advance and so that your boss can, too.

**SOLUTION:** Get tasks off your manager's desk and onto your desk. Be proactive in finding things that your boss is doing that you can handle for him or her. Coach your manager to focus on higher-impact activities and leave the rest to you. Tell your boss, "Help me help you." An organization in which everyone is pushing down responsibilities while reaching up for more responsibility is a very healthy one.

---

The best way to serve your boss or manager is to be everything that he or she is not. Your job is to protect your boss from blind spots and weaknesses. You need to understand how he or she operates and organize yourself and your skills in a way that is additive and complementary to every situation. If your boss is soft, then you have to be hard. If your boss won't delegate, then you have to proactively take work off his desk. Give your boss every opportunity to notice what an invaluable resource you are to the team, and make it impossible for him or her to imagine work without you.

**Wrap-up:** You are surrounded by BUTs. If you look at colleagues up, down, or across your organization, you see BUTs. They are everywhere. And when colleagues look at you they see your BUTs. It's time now for everyone to acknowledge and start talking about these BUTs so we can get ourselves organized around them. We all want to spend more time doing the things we like and the things we do skillfully. And we all want to spend less time doing the things we hate and the things we do poorly. This will only happen if we talk about our BUTs openly and honestly without shame or judgment. Let's drag them all out into the light and begin to manage them together. I'll cover your BUT and you cover mine is the modus operandi of healthy companies. It takes a village to raise a child, and it takes a village to manage all of our weaknesses and shortcomings. Let's create that village together.

# CHAPTER 5

# ALL BUTS ALL THE TIME

## THE BUT TALK

It is review time, and you walk into your boss's office and sit down at his meeting table. You say, "So tell me, what's my BUT?"

He says, "You actually have two BUTs I'd like to talk to you about. One is getting smaller, and the other is getting bigger. Your efforts to connect with your people and your displays of appreciation for their good work have been well received by them. If you can do more of that in one-on-one meetings versus the long, gushing emails, I think it will appear more authentic. With a little more effort, that BUT may disappear for good. The BUT I see growing is that you are becoming a bit of a drama queen."

You are absolutely stunned by your boss's words. However,

you read the earlier chapters of *Kiss Your BUT Good-bye*, and you know that a Truth Teller should never be interrupted. Your manager goes on: "You are overreacting to everyday problems and bringing drama to situations that should not have any. We pay you to put out fires, not to yell 'Fire!' I'm going to give you some recent examples of when your reactions made situations much worse than they actually were."

Wow! Now that's what we refer to as a kick-ass BUT-talk meeting. What we like about the BUT-talk concept is no matter how uncomfortable the issue, the employee and manager get right to the heart of the problem. We all have BUTs, so we might as well talk about them. Yes, the BUT term is silly and adolescent, but believe us, it works. It brings some levity to heavy topics and the emotions wrapped up in them. It's the ideal icebreaker for an employee review. Compare the term BUT to words like "weaknesses," "problems," "development needs," and "skill gaps." We would much prefer to have a BUT than any of those other words to describe our personal or professional failings. We think our managers also find it much easier to communicate with us honestly and openly if we are talking about our BUTs rather than those other things. We encourage you to try this BUT talk with your manager and your direct reports. We think everyone's review will be more productive, constructive, and revealing if they stay focused on the BUT.

## FULL DISCLOSURE

Although the case study above ended really well, in the world of BUTs and BUT management, sometimes there is no happy ending. Described below is the largest and most frustrating BUT in the universe. It cannot be tamed, shrunk, or covered because in the mind of its owner it simply does not exist.

---

## BUT BREAK: BEAVIS'S BUDDY
### "I repeatedly told Ray about his BUT, *but* he just doesn't get it."

A person has been told they have a BUT. They have been given specific examples of how that BUT manifests itself. It's been explained to them how the BUT is negatively impacting their colleagues. They have been told over and over again that if they can't shrink or cover this BUT, their career will be limited and/or their future with the firm will be short-lived. They have met repeatedly with their Truth Teller, and they have endured multiple BUT slaps and BUT talks.

The person continues to deny they have an issue, or they refuse to address it. They persist with the negative attitude or behaviors. They blame inept management for their lack of advancement. They ignore all of their Truth Teller's warnings, and they take no corrective action on the behaviors that are hurting the team.

What do we call someone like this? A BUT HEAD.

What do you do with someone like this?

You have to fire them!

**SOLUTION:** If you truly are a BUT HEAD, then even this book that we went to great lengths to write is unlikely to help you. You are too oblivious, too stubborn, or too proud to accept your troublesome imperfections. That's unfortunate for you, because these issues will follow you wherever you go. Please listen to your Truth Tellers and believe them before it is too late.

If you are the manager of a BUT HEAD, you need to understand that failure is an option. You can only do so much until such time as you realize that your time and effort are better spent on those colleagues who have a will to improve. You do the best you can to help people overcome their BUTs and be successful. If they throw the life preserver back at you, then it is he or she who chooses to drown in their own sea of self-delusion. You can only save people who want to be saved.

## A BUT CULTURE

Imagine a work environment where everyone on the team is acutely aware of their own BUT, their colleagues' BUT, and their boss's BUT. Everyone speaks freely about them and their personal efforts to shrink them. When BUTs do appear, they are summarily called out by colleagues, and the offender is made aware of their relapse. There is a deep commitment on the part of individuals to improve and a group-wide commitment to support every colleague in their betterment efforts. Picture a team armed with that information that organizes itself around the strengths and weaknesses of each of the team members. It then becomes a workplace where everyone spends more time in their areas of strength and less time in their areas of weakness. They can do that, because colleagues with the right skill set are covering their BUT, and they are doing the same for someone else. It becomes a team where all of the players are in the right position playing to all of their strengths. Think of the jump in team productivity when everyone is doing the activities they like and they are skilled in. What is the result? The team is better. Job satisfaction goes up. Employee turnover goes down. More is being produced with the same number of people. Productivity drives profitability and creates a winning team spirit that every talented job candidate would want to be a part of. Can a simple and playful word like BUT help create that type of vibrant and dynamic workplace culture? We think it can. And we hope you will help create a BUT culture in your business so that your team is more successful.

## BUT NOW WHAT?

The reading period is over. The moments of self-reflection have now passed. It's now go-time as it relates to your BUT and your career.

*We need you to do the ten things listed below and get to work on reshaping your BUT.*

1. Assess if your career is advancing as you had hoped. If you are dissatisfied with your progress, proceed to #2. (Even if you are satisfied with your career we suggest moving to #2, because you can always get better.)
2. Write down the BUTs you know you have. List them all. If you have more than ten, throw the book away and go see a therapist.

3. Go to your Truth Teller(s), and advise them you are on a quest to find your BUT. Give them your list, and ask them to add to it. Tell them to rank your BUTs in size order from largest to smallest and insist they walk you through each one with exquisite detail, however painful it may be. Ask a lot of questions, get clarification, request real-life examples, and take copious notes.

4. Share the Truth Teller's insights with the people who work most closely with you. Confirm the list is complete and accurate, and ask them to add any BUTs that were missed.

5. Now that you have an approved list of BUTs, go sit down with your manager and go over each of them. Confirm these are areas in which your manager would like to see you improve. Have your manager rank them, and focus on the two largest BUTS. Ask your manager to monitor your progress in shrinking these BUTS. Check back in every month for a quick assessment.

6. Make a highly visible commitment to improve. Announce to your colleagues, in whatever forum or venue you deem appropriate, the areas you know you need to improve. Request they help you make it happen by pointing out when your BUT is showing.

7. Aggressively seek out opportunities to work on your BUT. Put yourself in situations where, in the past, you failed because you were unaware of your personal flaw. Knowledge is power, and you have both now.

8. Identify and enlist colleagues who can help you cover your BUT. Chances are you will not be able to shrink all your

BUTs alone. Give them the tasks you don't like to do or don't have the aptitude for. Perhaps your colleagues have a few tasks they can hand over to you.

9. Ask the people around you what their BUTs are and how you can help them overcome them. Definitely ask your boss what his/her BUTs are so you can position yourself to help him or her stay focused on their areas of strength. Covering your boss's BUT is a win/win strategy.

10. Get everyone in your office involved in the BUT culture. Incite open and honest dialogue about everyone's BUT, and it will improve your work environment and lead to more productivity.

What are you waiting for? Get off your butt, and go kick some BUTs!

## BUT ENOUGH ALREADY!

Okay, we hear you. We are bringing this book in for a landing, and we hope you found the BUT concept interesting and at least mildly entertaining. If this book caused you to reflect on your own career and the behaviors you display at work, then in our eyes *Kiss Your BUT Good-Bye* has been a worthwhile read.

We buy a lot of business books, and we can honestly say that many are interesting, some are entertaining, but only a few are truly applicable and valuable. Almost every business book is way too long, given the handful of messages they are trying to relay. We tried to keep this book short and sweet so your most precious resource, time, could be used for other things.

We hope that somewhere in these pages you found your BUT. If we discussed your BUT, we hope you learned a little more about it and our suggestions for shrinking it or covering it will prove helpful. If we inspired you to search for a BUT not covered, that's good, too. Find your Truth Teller, and you will find your BUT. Whatever your BUT is, we hope you learned that you are not alone. Everyone has a BUT that, in some way, is holding them back. Those who have the courage to confront their BUT and manage it will be rewarded for their efforts and determination. Those who don't read this book and/or never find their BUT will never know why they didn't rise as fast and go as far in their careers as they had hoped. As silly as it sounds, we would like the BUT term and concept to find its way into the global business lexicon. If employees and their managers openly talk about their BUTs, the people, and the companies they work for, will become more productive and more profitable. If these BUT conversations lead to a BUT culture where everyone knows the strengths and weaknesses of every team member, then we have really created something special. We wish you luck in your search and your conquest.

# APPENDIX A

## A CASE STUDY IN BUT TALK

Here is a testimonial from Bob's colleague, who received a real-life BUT talk from Bob:

In the spring of 2010, my closest friend at work suggested that I stop by to see Bob Azelby, the national director of oncology sales, for some career advice. I wasn't sure what I would say or ask Bob, but I jumped at the opportunity to spend time with one of the company's senior sales executives. I was hopeful that I could finally sit down with someone in power who had an eye for sales and marketing talent and was in the position to put talent in the right place. I was unaware that my close friend who suggested the meeting told Bob that I needed a candid career discussion to identify the root cause of what was holding my career back.

At the time, I was growing increasingly anxious in my current role and I felt underutilized and underappreciated. In the prior two years, I had put my hat in the ring for seven different sales and marketing roles that would increase my influence, improve my ability to contribute, and position me for bigger and better things in the future. Unfortunately, I was zero for seven in getting that bigger job, and from my perspective it was becoming increasingly evident that there was something seriously wrong with my company and the leadership in the sales and marketing department. I was asking myself how a guy with my talent and experience could not advance in this organization.

I knew Bob, but not very well. He had a reputation for being candid and tough, but fair, and that's all I was looking for. I thought anyone with a sense of fairness would see that I have not been given the opportunities I deserved. I am an experienced, relentless, and confident sales and marketing executive, and I was certain that Bob would see it. At the very least, I wanted to start building a relationship with Bob, because he was in a position to hire talented people and potentially advance my career.

Remember, I was going into the meeting with the objective of networking and selling myself to Bob, while Bob's objective was to provide objective feedback and sound career advice. The meeting started well, with both of us exchanging pleasantries. I told him about my current career situation, my aspirations, and the extent of my frustration with our company. Bob asked me why I thought I was passed over for these roles. I said, "Corporate politics."

Bob looked puzzled and asked, "What do you think is the deep-rooted development issue that is holding you back?" Bob went on to candidly explain his personal development areas.

I acknowledged that I understood the question and then said, "It was my inability to manage up well."

"Manage up?" Bob said with disbelief. He then asked me what I thought was the objective of the meeting. I became very uncomfortable but was able to respond that I wanted to have a development discussion and get guidance on how I can approach my areas of weakness. Bob responded with "That's good to hear," and then asked, "Do you really think managing up is your critical development area?" I knew I was in trouble, but I wanted to be consistent so I answered yes. Bob responded "That is complete nonsense," and explained that if I didn't do some soul-searching to really understand and acknowledge my development areas, there was little hope of career advancement. Bob then looked me in the eye and said, "You are not as good as you think you are. And that's why you have not been promoted." He went on to say everyone has developmental areas that are holding them back, and if I did not think I had any, then I had the biggest development issue of all, no self-awareness. He went on to say that he did not know me well enough to give specifics, but he had a strong suspicion that I had a self-awareness problem.

I was crushed by those last words. I actually broke down in the meeting. While there's "no crying in baseball," there was crying that day in the biopharmaceutical business. I could not believe how delusional and oblivious I was to my situation and the reasons for it. It was me, not them!

Bob ended the meeting by pointing to my chest and saying, "I know there is a 'good guy' in there, and you just need to find him and let him out. Stop trying to be some phony hotshot sales and marketing executive, and let people get to know the real you."

I left the meeting stunned and upset but knew deep down he was right. After deep introspection and working through the five stages of processing my BUTs, I accepted that I had developed several BUTs during the prior three years:

I developed a "Bitch and Moan" defense mechanism.

I developed an "Idiot Syndrome" combined with a "Wasn't-Me" attitude.

I failed to "Finish First" in my two prior roles.

There is no doubt that I received the much-needed BUT slap of my career, and I was thrown a life preserver. Bob let me know I could be saved if I wanted to be.

I am happy to report that after a lot more introspection, I got a handle on all of my BUTs and began the hard work of shrinking them. I was soon on the road to recovery but fully aware that some of my BUTs may reappear if not managed properly. I just completed my most successful year with four of my direct reports being promoted. I also received a standing ovation at our national sales meeting from seven hundred of my colleagues who are getting to know the real me now that I know the real me. I have transitioned into a much broader international role, and my career is back on track.

The best advice I can give people is go find your Truth Teller and listen to him or her. Take it all in, and then get to work fixing it. You have to own your BUTs to shrink your BUTs. Like me, you'll have everything to gain and nothing to lose.

# APPENDIX B

## CONCEPT SUMMARY

## THE BUT

This is what we're talking about.

- Jim is a great salesman, *but* he can't close.
- Rachel works hard, *but* she can't prioritize.
- Larry is a great producer, *but* he's arrogant.
- Lisa has plenty of IQ, *but* she has no EQ.

In our experience, the major reason people's careers do not advance is that they are either lacking a skill or have a behavior that either disqualifies them or renders them less qualified than other candidates. Take ownership of your career, and remember that your situation is a result of the actions and behaviors that you control. They are your BUTs.

## YOU HAVE A BUT

We guarantee you that in hallways and conference rooms your BUT is being discussed. People just love talking about your BUT, especially your peers, who take every opportunity to bring it up. Your colleagues are having too much fun with your BUT to tell you about it. They know if they disclose your BUT to you that you may stop exposing it to them and others. In some cases, they want your BUT to hold you back so they can advance and you won't.

## FINDING YOUR BUT

If a Truth Teller is willing to talk to you about your BUT, you had better listen closely. When the Truth Teller is providing feedback on your BUT and how you can improve, you must accept the feedback even though you are struggling with it. Listen to what is said outright, and also listen for important messages that may be too hurtful for your Truth Teller to verbalize but are intimated in other ways. Even if you disagree with the Truth Teller's feedback, accept it at face value. It does not matter what you think of yourself, but rather what other people think of you. Their perception of you is your reality whether you like it or not.

If you are fortunate enough to find a manager or Truth Teller to give it to you straight, we want to make sure you are emotionally prepared for what you may be told. If it's a big, ugly, BUT you will feel pain right down into your heart and soul. Once your BUT has been exposed to you, it's critically important that you stare at it and acknowledge it. You must understand the impact it is having on you, your subordinates, peers, customers, and your manager. By discovering, staring at, and most importantly accepting your BUT, you can begin to manage it.

## WHIPPING YOUR BUT

You can't fool people when it comes to your BUT. They will see right through a token effort or the slightest insincerity regarding the steps you are taking to fix the problem. The commitment to change must come from deep within you if you are to sell it to those who have suffered from your BUT. Shrinking your BUT is all about checking your ego at the door and making a sincere and concerted effort to be an effective professional and a better employee. You must look for and anticipate opportunities where you can work on your BUT and seek out situations where you can show the world you are confronting it.

Partner with people in your office who are very strong in the areas where you are weak. When you spend time with these people, you will realize they too have weaknesses, and in many cases their weaknesses may actually be your areas of strength. Once you know your BUT, find those individuals who can complement it, and always look for situations where you can return the favor.

## YOUR MANAGER'S BUT

Like you, your boss has a BUT, or in some cases many BUTs. You need to spend time analyzing and understanding your boss's BUTs and determine which are the largest and most visible. It's critically important you understand where your boss is weak and vulnerable and position your unique skills to cover these BUTs. If your strengths offset your boss's weaknesses you will be a very valued employee.

## BUT NOW WHAT?

We need you to do the ten things listed below and get to work on reshaping your BUT.

1. Assess if your career is advancing as you had hoped. If not, proceed to #2.
2. Write down the BUTs you know you have.
3. Go to your Truth Teller(s), give them your list, and ask them to add to it.
4. Share the Truth Teller's insights with your coworkers to confirm the list is complete and accurate.
5. Sit down with your manager and go over each BUT. Have your manager rank them and commit to focusing on the two largest BUTs.
6. Announce to your colleagues the areas you need to improve, and request their help.
7. Aggressively seek out opportunities to work on your BUT.
8. Enlist colleagues who can help you cover your BUT, and give them the tasks you don't like to do or have no aptitude for.

9. Ask your boss as well as the people around you what their BUTs are and how you can help them overcome them.

10. Get everyone in your office involved in the BUT culture by inciting open and honest dialogue about everyone's BUT.

# APPENDIX C

---

## BUTS BY APB

**B**elow you will find a long list of BUTs associated with aptitude, personality, and behavior. Some BUTs you'll recognize from the main text, and other BUTs are brand-new. We have given some of them code names to help you remember them. They were written for you and about you. We start by describing how colleagues think and feel about people with each BUT. We also cover the actions you should take to shrink, cover, or eliminate them. Read and internalize each description so you can manage the BUTs you have and avoid developing the ones you don't. BUTs are not exclusive to one of the three buckets, so our groupings should be used only as a guide. If you think we are too harsh, we say, "You're welcome." We want to get your attention before you develop a bad case of one of these.

# APTITUDE

**Analyze This!: " . . . but has weak analytical skills." (see page 24)**

You can do the math, but you can't ascertain what the numbers are telling you.

Business is a numbers game. The top players are adept at studying the figures and identifying the patterns and trends that highlight the important risks and opportunities inherent in the business. There are a lot of smart people who can "crunch" the numbers but simply can't interpret them. Analytical skills are part art and part science, mixed in with a lot of experience. If you can't do the math/science part then you probably picked the wrong job. If you can't identify the important trends, you need more experience and mentoring from those who can.

**Solution:** If you have been given feedback that weak analytical skills is your BUT, you should take it very seriously. If you can't do the math part, you can't do the job. Go look for a new role. Interpreting the numbers is equally important. Some people have an intuitive gift for this, and others develop it over time. Cover this BUT by taking a course on Excel or other analytical software. Go retake the statistics class you did poorly in at college. Find the people in your company with strong analytical skills and ask them to mentor you. Reserve a conference room. Bring in lunch and get the experts to take you through their thought processes.

**New—A to Y: " . . . but cannot execute from end to end."**

You start a lot of projects, but you finish very few. Execution is the ability to plan, start, and finish tasks. You have trouble doing all three, and you end up with a lot of half-finished or abandoned projects. The ability to execute is the key to business success. You have to get things done and do them well. With this BUT, the closer you get to project completion, the harder things get. That's why so many more projects are started than finished. You can plan and start a project, but if you can't execute from end to end and successfully complete it, you have a problem.

**Solution:** If execution is your BUT, you need to shrink it or cover it. To shrink it, you must mentally commit to finishing every project you start. Don't take on another project until the first one is done. It is so much easier starting projects than finishing them. Grind your way to completion on the first project before even thinking about a second project. If you have to cover your BUT, then partner with someone with the project management skills and tenacity to close out projects. Take the finished product to your manager and confirm it's complete. Then make a very public announcement thanking everyone who helped you.

### New—The Bigger Picture: " . . . but struggles to think strategically."

You are good at tasks but have little understanding of what your company is trying to achieve. Make no mistake about it, Bigger Picture = Bigger Paychecks. If people say you can't see the forest through the trees, or that you win battles but lose the war, it's a problem. Putting your head down and getting things done is laudable but insufficient. Strategic thinking is seeing beyond the present and beyond your narrow function and understanding what your company in its entirety is trying to become.

**Solution:** You must learn to execute on urgent stuff while at all times knowing the important strategic issues your company faces. Urgent things have to be done today, while important things, such as seeing the future, need to be worked on every day. You need to read the trade journals, meet with industry luminaries, and study the competition. Lift up your head and try to understand where your clients and your industry are going, and get there before they do.

### The Blind Side: " . . . but she has a blind spot with one of her direct reports." (see page 126)

You fail to properly and accurately assess people and situations from your vantage point. Every person, at some point in time, has a blind side, in that he or she may not be able to see everything that's going on in the group from their perspective. Risks may be developing in the business you cannot see. There may be someone on the team who is underperforming or damaging the group's culture. You may be so focused on your traditional competitor that you completely ignore the upstart company that is starting to steal your clients.

**Solution:** Use *The Blind Side* movie analogy in your team discussions. Explain to everyone that they all have to be vigilant "left tackles" always on the lookout for threats to the business or the culture. Start or end your meetings with the following question: "Does anyone see something that we may not see that is creating risks to our business? If so, say it now or come see me later."

### New—Coffee is for Closers: " . . . but can't close new business."

Clients like you. You have a full calendar of meetings. But you don't produce good sales numbers. If you are a salesperson and you cannot close business, you are of little value to your company. Salespeople have to get the customer to sign on the dotted line and buy the product or service. The survival of the company depends on it. The people who can do that consistently are worth their weight in gold. Those who cannot don't get coffee or a paycheck.

**Solution:** To learn the art of the close, you need to spend time with the most senior and most productive salespeople in your company. Selling is part science and part art. If your company has a sales culture, they will give you the tools to master the science. Attend the sales training classes and increase your aptitude. Just as important, shadow the grand masters at your company who consistently put up big sales numbers, so you can learn the art side of selling. They will show you the secret of knowing exactly when and how to ask the client for the business. You only get what you ask for and the grand masters know how to ask.

### New—Comma Chameleon: " . . . but cannot write."

Your memos and emails are long, boring, and off point. Despite all the technological changes, writing is still the most common form of communication. Therefore, you must be able to write clearly and concisely if you want to be successful. You don't need to be Hemingway or Shakespeare, but you do need to provide facts, opinions, and analysis in a coherent written form. In today's world of emails, texts, and Twitter, written communication is more important than ever.

**Solution:** Practice your writing. Take a business-writing course. Get a capable colleague to edit your work before it's released to the public. If written communication is your BUT, shrink it, cover it, or complement it as soon as possible.

### Comfy: " . . . but has grown complacent." (see page 80)

You have been in your job too long, and you have lost your edge; you are too comfortable with how things work. The people, process, and culture have a familiar rhythm to them that has lulled you into a state of complacency. World markets, industry competitors, and your customers are anything but complacent. If you are a leader in an organization and you are not preparing for and adapting to a very different future, you'd better get moving or you'll be moved out.

**Solution:** You need a wake-up call. Get out of your office, and talk to the people on the front lines. Find out what is working and what is not. Hire somebody from your biggest competitor so they can show how and why things are done differently there. Rival companies are like snipers waiting to get off a clear shot at you and your company. Know where they are and exactly what they are doing.

### New—Control What You Can Control: " . . . but is not buttoned up."

You don't do the administrative tasks your job requires. Not delivering on the simple job requirements (e.g., expense reports, client call memos, and business updates) is like getting straight A's in advanced calculus, organic chemistry, and quantum physics, and then failing to graduate because you did not fulfill your physical education requirement. You need to understand that if you don't execute and deliver on these basic things your colleagues and your boss will lose confidence in you. You must consistently and accurately perform the administrational aspects of your position.

**Solution:** Tasks, such as submitting travel receipts, attending compliance training, and filling out self-assessments, are the corporate equivalent of personal hygiene. You just have to get these things done, no matter how busy you think you are. Do your annual self-assessment. Get your compliance-training course completed. Make a list of these tasks, put them on your calendar, and get them done. If organizational skills and attention to detail are not your strengths, you had better find a way to cover that BUT. It could be as simple as hiring a compulsively organized assistant.

### New—First Things First: " . . . but can't prioritize."

You don't know which tasks are the most important, so you reactively jump from one to the other. Business is all about delivering a high-quality finished product to customers at a good price. Inside companies your colleagues are your customers. You must build a personal brand of delivering high-quality work in the shortest amount of time possible. Time is the currency of companies, and you want to use it as effectively and efficiently as possible, while always maintaining high quality.

**Solution:** Finish the task at hand before starting the next one. Overreaching leads to shoddy work and late delivery. Both will destroy your personal brand. The best way to prevent this BUT from growing is to have the courage to say no. Some people have trouble staying focused on the highest priorities when people show up asking for help. Every day write a task list in priority order and do not start item #2 until item #1 is finished.

### Groundhog Day: " . . . but I can't picture him doing anything else." (see page 87)

You have a narrow job focus, and you like that. There is nothing wrong with being a focused expert. The risk you run is that colleagues and management may pigeonhole you into that very specific function. This can really limit your ability to be promoted or moved to a new business line with better growth prospects. If you find that you are doing much the same thing every day, then you are probably not growing professionally. If the world changes, which we know it will, you could be at risk of losing your job.

**Solution:** If you are happy doing what you are doing, then focus all of your energy and expertise on making sure that you remain the very best in that chosen field. Be mindful, of course, that there could be major market disruptions or technology advances in your area that can potentially make you obsolete. To hedge this risk, show your company that you have more to offer. Go to an industry event and get on a panel discussion to highlight your passion for the subject and your communication skills. Go with your salespeople to a client meeting and help win the deal. Get involved in projects and committees that will give you profile and an opportunity to contribute in new ways.

### New—Holy Moses: " . . . but is unable to persuade."

You stink at convincing people your ideas are good ones. The ability to influence and persuade others is a skill requirement for people in leadership positions. We define leadership as the ability to create a future that would not have happened anyway. To achieve an unanticipated and better future, a leader and salesperson must convince people to follow him or her into the desert. You have to sell your ideas to colleagues in order to get them to change from what they are currently doing. Good ideas are not enough. Getting people to risk what they have today in exchange for what they can get tomorrow requires a keen ability to persuade.

**Solution:** If this is your BUT, spend time watching people who are able to move the organization in ways not thought possible. Ask them how they do it, and then watch them do it. "Influence" and "persuasion" are just fancy words for selling skills. The only difference is that you are selling to colleagues rather than clients. In both situations you must convince someone that your idea or your vision will in some way improve their life.

### King of Pain: " . . . but must expand comfort zone." (see page 90)

You don't like doing things you have never done before. It's called a comfort zone because you feel perfectly relaxed and confident within it. You have completed the tasks in your comfort zone many times before. Moving outside of that zone involves risk, learning, changing, pain, and misery. To get better, go further, and grow both personally and professionally, you should crave circumstances and assignments that are outside your comfort zone. You grow the most when you are stretched to the limits of your skills, talents, and pain threshold. Companies want pain and misery for their most promising managers, because it makes them grow and makes them better.

**Solution:** You must be willing to seek stretch assignments. Ask for new roles or projects that will challenge you. Make sure you do some things at work that make your palms sweat.

### Premature Self-Adulation (PSA): " . . . but has not mastered the current job." (see page 104)

You think you are a lot better than you are. You have not mastered your current role, so you should not be asking for a promotion. This is commonplace among young professionals who have graduated from top-notch schools, as well as other ambitious employees. No good manager is going to give you a bigger and better job until you have mastered your current role.

**Solution:** If you want a new job, you should be doing the current job better than others who have done it before. The job you want to leave should be bigger, broader, and more complex than the job you were first given. Until you have done all that, do not ask your manager or anyone else in the organization about your want or need for career advancement. Ask your manager what you need to do to get to the next level, and then go do it.

**New—Public Misspeaking: " . . . but has terrible presentation skills."**

You cringe when you have to get up in front of an audience, and so does the audience. Nervousness, hemming and hawing, monotone voice, and standing as if one's feet are nailed to the floor are just a few signs that you are not ready for prime-time presentations. Companies place a lot of emphasis on presentation skills because communicating information is the key to most companies' success.

**Solution:** If this is the issue holding you back, ask your company to send you to training. There are methods and techniques to presenting that will make you better once you know them. If the company won't pay for presentation training, then pay for it yourself. It's a great investment with a very high return. Enhancing your presentation skills can be done with professional help and plenty of practice.

**New—Silence of the Lambs: " . . . but needs to ask more questions."**

You sit quietly in conference rooms and never raise your hand. Your boss tells you to do something, and you are not exactly sure what he or she wants. You don't circle back and ask for clarification. Not asking questions can be a derailing handicap in any corporation. Be curious. Be brave. People love to show you how much they know, so give them the opportunity to do so. Check your ego, pride, or insecurity at the door of every office and conference room, and ask a lot of questions. Hiding your ignorance is the most effective way to perpetuate it.

**Solution:** On the next project, develop a better understanding of how this project fits into the broader company strategy so you can adjust the project properly as more information is acquired. Ask proactive, open-ended questions so that your manager can clarify exactly what is needed from you or your team. Asking questions shows confidence, interest, and engagement.

### New—No Report Card: " . . . but never gives feedback."

You never tell your people exactly where they stand and where they need to go. You never take the time to provide your staff members valuable feedback. It's one of the most important responsibilities you have, and you choose to neglect it. How can an employee or a team get better if you do not tell them how they are doing?

**Solution:** If you manage people, you have an obligation to give them feedback, and they have an inalienable right to receive it from you. Feedback is like homemade bread. It is best served hot and fresh. Never wait to give feedback. It must be delivered and received right after the incident, meeting, or presentation. That is the point of maximum courage and receptivity for the giver and taker. Two days later the feedback is stale and more difficult to digest. Give feedback as soon as possible. Jump at the chance to be your colleague's Truth Teller.

**Sooner Rather than Later: " . . . but takes too long to deliver the final product." (see page 85)**

You do not deliver things in the time frame they are needed. If you have this BUT, you may be a perfectionist who will not deliver your work until it is thoroughly and flawlessly completed. That's great, but clients and markets don't wait for perfection. They need solutions, and they need them now. Sometimes "good enough" today wins out over "perfect" tomorrow.

Solution: You can always provide fewer details in your report, or ask your manager for more lead time on a project. Find out exactly what is needed and by when. Strike the proper balance between content, time, and effort. There is a great business term we recently learned: ALAPAMAN. Remember this term. It stands for As Little As Possible . . . As Much As Necessary. The most productive and efficient employees consistently deliver ALAPAMAN.

# PERSONALITY

**Anger Management: " . . . but he gets so angry over trivial things." (see page 25)**

You are a hothead who flies off the handle. Nobody likes an angry man or woman. The yelling, cursing, and the aggressive posture are really unattractive. If you think that an apology after an angry outburst sets things right, you are dead wrong. Angry outbursts leave people battered and scarred. People don't like or trust those who are unpredictably explosive. Remember, if you are a time bomb, your company will first defuse you and then dispose of you.

**Solution:** Get a grip on your anger. Focus on who or what incites that anger, and do everything you can to avoid that person or situation. An angry outburst makes you feel better for a minute and makes everyone around you feel bad for a month. Remember that most anger is driven by fear. You think you are being tough when in reality you're just scared.

**Arrogance Defined: " . . . but appears arrogant." (see page 106)** Everyone thinks that you are a stuck-up snob. You only have time for people more senior than you. You talk down to everyone else. You speak with an extreme authoritative tone laced with sarcasm. When colleagues describe someone as arrogant, they are basically saying they don't like or trust that person. "Arrogant" is a catch-all label that is devastating to the employee it is bestowed upon. If your manager has told you that you are perceived as arrogant, you have a lot of work to do.

**Solution:** You must become more like the people around you so they can identify with you. Most important, take an interest in their lives. Ask them questions about things that are important to them. Let them waste a few company minutes sharing with you their fears and passions. There is no playbook for removing the arrogance BUT. However, if you are opening up to people and encouraging them to open up with you, we guarantee they will like you and trust you a little more than they did before.

### New—Condescension: " . . . but is so condescending."

You talk to people as if they are your servants. Using a tone of superiority when speaking to people less powerful than you will not be well received. Human history and corporate offices are littered with people who became intoxicated with their power and oppressed the people who helped put them there in the first place. It pays to treat everyone with respect, especially the people who look to you for leadership. You must always be engendering two-way loyalty and commitment with your team. They are the people who will determine your success and they will be the people who come to your rescue during difficult times. The most effective way to destroy goodwill with them is to talk to them in a condescending manner.

**Solution:** Watch your tone. Be respectful. Speak to people the way you want to be spoken to. Address the security guard and the cleaning lady in the same manner you speak with your peers. If you talk with a condescending tone, people will think you are a jerk—and they'll probably be right.

### Down and Out: " . . . but is not resilient." (see page 63)

You don't bounce back from failures and disappointments. You mope around the office with that sullen "woe is me" look. Setbacks and disappointments are part of the business life and you are judged by how you respond and recover from them. Business is like boxing, in that you take some big hits during your career, and at times you will find yourself on the canvas.

**Solution:** Self-pity and blaming others is a waste of valuable time. The best thing to do is get up and fight on. What doesn't kill you will make you stronger. And as long as you keep fighting, you always have a chance to win. The next time you have a setback at work, you must think about it as an educational opportunity and learn from it. Positive energy is the best response to a negative event.

### The Egomaniac: " . . . but has a huge ego." (see page 119)

You think it's all about you. You view yourself as so important that your bad behavior is simply the price of having your talent around. You are so valuable that the rules of the firm and society more broadly simply do not apply to you. You are often disrespectful of senior management and show disdain for the company. You look for every opportunity to put your wants, needs, and ambitions before those of your colleagues and the company.

**Solution:** If you are the egomaniac, we do not have any advice for you except to tone it down or leave the company. It's not about you, and we can all live without you. If you are the egomaniac's manager, it's time for you to take action. Your people are watching the egomaniac closely, and they are watching your reaction and response to the situation even more closely.

**New—Idiot Syndrome: " . . . but they think everyone else is an idiot."**

You think you are the greatest person in the company and that everyone else is a lazy dimwit. People with idiot syndrome are often very talented, but in their mind, the people who manage them and support them are idiots. You tell people how amazing it is that you alone can accomplish all that you do, given how incompetent everyone else is.

**Solution:** Treat everyone in your firm like they are your client. Why? Because your colleagues are just like your clients. They decide if you are someone with whom they would like to do business. They decide if your priority should be their priority. They decide if they should help you or some other salesperson out in the field. You have to compete with other firms to win business. You also have to compete internally for the help and support of your colleagues.

**Inauthentic: " . . . but is perceived as a phony." (see page 73)**

People think you are as phony as a three-dollar bill. If colleagues view you as manipulative or conniving, that is a big problem. You speak and act with a specific personal agenda in mind. You are viewed as inauthentic, and you are not trusted. Your colleagues know that your personal agenda is far more important to you than the company's agenda.

**Solution:** Being perceived as inauthentic is really tough to overcome. The first thing you have to do is decide if your goals and ambitions are the same as the company's. Then you have to decide if you are willing to partner with your colleagues to achieve a shared level of success. If you can do those two things, your career with the company is salvageable. You will need to show people the success of the team is more important than your personal success.

**Jekyll and Hyde: " . . . but is so moody." (see page 21)**

Your personality and demeanor are volatile and erratic. Nobody wants to work with a moody person. One day you are pleasant and cooperative and the next day you are hostile and belligerent. You can set a bad tone for the day as soon as you enter a room. You are like an improvised explosive device that can destroy the morale of an entire team. Your bipolar antics cause everyone else to walk on eggshells, and you prevent work from getting done.

**Solution:** If you are the moody person, don't bring your emotional baggage to work. Avoid people and situations that set you off. Smile on the outside, even if you are a raving maniac on the inside. People who are well balanced and can manage the stress and strains of their professional and personal lives are those who can lead. Additionally, if you are a manager of others, you have to be extra careful about your mood, because its impact can be devastating. If people look up to you for leadership, keep it on an even keel. If you can't control your mood, then limit your contact with others on those bad days.

**Master of the Oblivious: " . . . but has no self-awareness."
(see page 135)**

You are oblivious to the fact that people are reacting badly to you even when you've been told many times. You have been told that you have a BUT. You have been given specific examples of how that BUT manifests itself. It's been explained to you how your BUT is negatively impacting your colleagues. You have been told repeatedly if you can't shrink or cover this BUT your career will be limited and/or your future with the firm short-lived. You repeatedly deny you have a problem. You continue with the negative attitude or behaviors. You blame inept management for your lack of advancement. You ignore all of your Truth Teller's warnings. And you take no corrective action.

**Solution:** You have to know and understand how people are responding to you. Self-awareness is the most important quality for any business professional. Without it you are flying without radar in a blinding thunderstorm. If you can't pick up negative response signals from others on your own, then you need to get help before you crash. That is why Truth Tellers are important and why listening to them is even more important. If you have been told you have no self-awareness, go buy a book on self-awareness. Or just read this one again. Both will teach you to listen for the signals you have missed for so long. Accept what your Truth Teller says.

**Mean Reversion: " . . . but has a mean streak." (see page 69)**
You can be a mean-spirited jerk who will purposely hurt people

who don't deserve it. Attacking colleagues and damaging their egos and reputations is what meanness looks like in the workplace. If you are perceived as mean, everything you say and do thereafter will be seen through that lens. People will not follow you. They will fear you, but they will not follow you. If people see that you are mean to others, they are rightfully certain you will be mean to them someday, whether they are present for the attack or not. People will organize themselves quickly against someone they perceive as mean.

**Solution:** We don't have any great advice on how to overcome a deserved reputation for meanness. Nothing short of a complete mea culpa and a sincere effort to change your ways will work. If afterward you revert to being mean, even once, they will come for you, and you will be taken out.

### Mr. Brightside: " . . . but is delusional." (see page 16)

You are not taken seriously, because you never confront reality. You believe that happy thoughts will solve problems. While optimism is a wonderful personal characteristic, it needs to be grounded in some basic realities. A business will not improve or become more competitive just by wishing or saying it will. If you are always optimistic without a strategy or actions to justify your optimism, you will lose credibility with your colleagues and managers.

**Solution:** Be realistic at all times. If you have problems, talk about them, and deal with them. If you see opportunities, lay out the specific steps that need to be taken to capture them. Provide specific facts and measurable trends that underpin the

reasons for your optimism. Show people that you have a balanced view of the risks and rewards your business faces and
manages every day.

### New—The Ogre: " . . . but comes across as intimidating."

You are scary. You are gruff, terse, and have a scowl on your
face. You are easily annoyed and at times excessively aggressive. You keep your door closed and you only meet with people
who have made appointments well in advance. You send signals to everyone that they should approach you with caution.

**Solution:** Ask the people close to you if you are perceived
as approachable. If they say no, then you are probably intimidating. Don't wait for people to engage you. They are afraid.
You need to engage them. Lighten up. Smile at people. Talk
about the weather or the local sports team on the elevator. Tell
an embarrassing story about yourself at the next team event.

### The PAB (Passive-Aggressive Behavior): " . . . but is passive-aggressive." (see page 82)

You are subversive and covertly insubordinate when you don't
want to do something. You fight against change and management without ever engaging them directly. You are a corporate guerrilla fighting a losing battle. You have some passive-
aggressive tendencies, and it has become your modus operandi.
It's a coping mechanism and survival skill that has been honed
by humans over the last few hundred thousand years. When
you do not want to do something you have been told to do,
you go to great lengths not to do it while never saying that you

won't do it. You do everything you can to resist change without ever publicly protesting the change.

**Solution:** We all have been passive-aggressive at some point in our work life. It's okay to resist, as long as you do it quickly and quietly. Go to your manager. If you listen to the reasoning behind the decision, perhaps it will be easier to accept the decision. Express your concerns about the changes and perhaps those changes will be adjusted based on your feedback. Sooner or later you have to get on the bus. We recommend getting on the bus sooner rather than later, because you will get a much better seat.

### Replaceable Part: " . . . but he believes he is irreplaceable." (see page 6)

You believe that your team cannot survive without you. The moment you start believing that you can't be replaced is the beginning of the end. We are all replaceable, and we should never forget it. There is a talented colleague in your company who would love to have your job. And there is an army of talent in the market looking for good jobs like yours. If you act like you are irreplaceable, you may come to the office one day and find all of your personal effects packed up and a new name plaque on the door.

**Solution:** Never let up. Compete every day. Be paranoid about the competition. The more knowledgeable and productive you are, the more difficult you are to replace.

**New—Touch of Gray: " . . . but only sees the world in black-and-white."**

You make snap judgments based only on high-level surface information. You pride yourself on seeing the world and situations as either black or white. The reality is that not every situation is black or white. Many are subtle, nuanced, or very complicated. Seeing the world in black-and-white and deciding accordingly is fast and simple. However, the decisions you make on that basis are more often wrong than right.

**Solution:** Leaders need to explore the gray area before reaching conclusions. Understand the details. Know what information was available at the time. Assess the external influences. Appreciate everyone's state of mind. Managers who do their due diligence before acting make better decisions. A touch of gray in your hair makes you look wiser. A touch of gray in your assessments and decision making will help you be wiser.

**Why So Serious? " . . . but he needs to lighten up."**
**(see page 42)**

People think you are a humorless corporate tool. You never smile. You are always in a hurry. You are short and terse in all interactions. You are so much busier than everyone else, and the weight of the world sits squarely on your shoulders. Watching your pulsating carotid artery and bulging temple veins as you breathlessly describe the challenges of the technology upgrade initiative does not inspire confidence. In fact, it leaves people feeling both nervous and exhausted.

**Solution:** Lighten up. You can smile once in a while and engage a colleague in conversation that has nothing to do with the bottom line. Take down the intensity a few notches, and the work will still get done. Athletes and workers who are focused and relaxed play better and work better than those who are nervous and stressed.

## BEHAVIOR

### The Abyss: " . . . but won't respond to my calls or emails." (see page 112)

You are unresponsive. Messages go into the cold, dark abyss, but they don't come out. A deadline is looming. Your input is either wanted or needed. After numerous attempts, hours, days, or weeks pass with dead silence.

**Solution:** You have an obligation to respond to your colleagues. If an answer or acknowledgment is needed, do it as soon as you read the email or listen to the voice mail. If the response requires some thought, just write, "Got it, I'll be back to you ASAP." Put a note on your calendar if you are prone to forgetting these types of commitments.

### The Arguer: " . . . but is argumentative." (see page 46)

You turn discussions into fights. You love to argue, and you approach any disagreement as a full-contact sport. You feel that if someone has a view that is different from your own, that view and its owner must be summarily destroyed. The person who disagrees with you must submit to an unconditional surrender of their position.

**Solution:** Issues can be discussed without there being an argument. People can disagree without attacking each other. The strength of the reasoning behind a position is more powerful than the loud voice or the aggressive lean-in across the conference table. You don't have to win every argument. Let the other person win, or declare it a draw. While it's a lame phrase, "Let's agree to disagree" will be an improvement over your current practice. Change your approach, or you will not have anyone left to argue with.

### New—Back-Channel Charlie: " . . . he bcc's everyone on what should be confidential emails."

You invite people into your email conversations without letting the other person know. The bcc moniker on your email system also stands for "Being Covertly Contemptible." It's surreptitious and downright creepy to secretly invite other people into what appears to be a one-on-one communication. When is it proper to send someone an email and simultaneously send it to other people without the recipient knowing who else is watching? Probably . . . never. Would you schedule a phone call with someone and then invite others in the room to listen to the speakerphone conversation without telling the other person who was there? We hope not.

**Solution:** Stop using the bcc function. Make it a personal policy to never use it again. If you can't show the recipient of your email all of the people seeing the email, then you are being dishonest. Disarm and disavow your bcc function, and you will be glad you did.

**New—Bad-News Bear: " . . . but overreacts to bad news."**

You get really upset when people bring you bad news. Showing anger, fear, or panic when colleagues bring you bad news only makes the situation worse. It also discourages them from telling you things you need to know. Okay, so your largest client has informed you they will be using another vendor. Dramatically expressing how this loss could lead to other business and financial problems will create an imaginary abominable snowball of disaster that will scare the hell out of everybody. Bad things happen in business. Get used to it.

**Solution:** The bigger the problem the more important it is to modulate your reaction. We like the following phrase when receiving bad news: "Is that so?" It has a calming effect on the situation by keeping the possibility alive that the decision could be reversed or the situation resolved favorably. Afterward, listen intently. Get all of the facts. Be calm and ask a lot of questions. Be sure to profusely thank the messenger. This helps ensure that other bad-news messengers will come to you. Now that you have the information, focus only on the immediate problem and try to solve it. In this case, call the client. Find out why they are dropping your product or service. Explore ways to save the business, or at least part of it. Cool heads prevail in challenging situations.

**Beat Your Boss to the Punch: " . . . but needs constant follow-up." (see page 100)**

You don't keep important people updated. The boss gave you an assignment five weeks ago and has not heard from you since.

When you have the opportunity to lead a really meaningful project, make sure you update your manager before they ask you for an update. Most managers in today's working world are swamped with issues and struggle to stay updated on their important projects. When people do not check in, managers stress out because they naturally assume the project is not on track and that the project manager may be hiding something from them. The most successful people in an organization know how often their managers want to be updated and they always make sure they beat that time line by a few days or a few hours.

**Solution:** There is a simple solution to this challenge, and it's one that many people overlook. Ask your boss how often they would like to be updated. Every boss is different, so why hazard a guess? Even with that information, you still have to make sure you inform your manager prior to their requesting an update. Managers hate surprises. The more you ask on the front end and the more you communicate along the way, the less likely there will be any surprises on the back end.

**New—Bitch and Moan: " . . . but complains about everything."**
You are a miserable malcontent. You just suck the energy out of a team because all you do is complain. The worst thing about you is that when you are in front of your managers or senior executives, you are saying everything is going great and how much you love the company. You think you are a smooth operator, and you believe you know how to work the system. The truth of the matter is that everybody in the organization realizes you are an unappreciative, self-centered jerk.

**Solution:** Think of all the time and energy that you waste by complaining. If you could take that energy and apply it to solving the issues that bother you so much, both you and your colleagues would enjoy your jobs so much more. The company would also benefit because your help finding solutions will enable the company to be more productive and likely more profitable. Every time you feel the urge to complain just ask yourself, "What can I do to make this situation better?" If you ask that question and act on the answer, we guarantee that you will change the trajectory of your career for the better.

**The Bored of Directors: " . . . but he does not consistently engage like his peers." (see page 113)**

When you get bored in a meeting, you sign off without telling anybody. You write emails on your smartphone. You doodle on a notepad. You sit there silently thinking about all the things you could be getting done. You sleep with your eyes open—and occasionally with your eyes closed.

**Solution:** Do not disengage when you get bored in meetings. If you are bored, chances are the other people in the room are also bored. You can be the hero by getting the meeting back on track and getting everyone to focus on the most important issues or driving the group to get to a decision. Ask important questions such as "Did everyone read the material?" "Then why are we going through it?" "Are there questions on the material?" "Are we here to make a decision, or is this just informational?" "What does the presenter need from this committee?" These types of questions will help make the meetings shorter, more focused, and more likely to lead to a decision or action.

### The BPU: " . . . but is considered an obstructionist."
### (see page 37)

You are adamantly opposed to change. Obstructionists (members of the Business Prevention Unit) like you do their very best to kill any new idea or initiative that diverges from the normal course of business. You are heavily invested in the status quo and you do everything necessary to preserve it. You will use scare tactics and raise concerns or issues that are often difficult to quantify or deflect, in an effort to derail any proposed change or new initiative. You use an arsenal of ominous terms like "business risk," "reputation risk," "franchise risk," "regulatory risk," or "litigation risk" to scare the hell out of the decision-making body.

**Solution:** If you are perceived as an obstructionist, this BUT will limit your advancement. To shrink this BUT you must be open to new ideas. Explore potential innovations with energy and enthusiasm. Support some new initiatives and constructively look for ways to make them work. Help the organization move toward the future, rather than living in the past.

### Cape Fear: " . . . but can't pull the trigger." (see page 51)

You are slow and hesitant to take action. You know what needs to be done, but you are afraid to do it. You obsess over the things that might go wrong if you act, rather than seeing how the situation will improve once you take action. If you are perceived as fearful or insecure and unable to take action in challenging situations, it's unlikely that you will be given more responsibility. And it is quite likely that you will be given less responsibility. An inability to act is an inability to lead.

**Solution:** Once you know what needs to be done, do it quickly and decisively. Your colleagues are watching. They know what you need to do, and every day that you wait you lose some of their confidence in you. If necessary, confide in a trusted colleague and get assurance that you are doing the right thing. Action beats inaction when dealing with problems. Be bold.

### New—Counterfeit Answers: " . . . but tries to fake it."

When you don't have the answer you make something up. You are making a big presentation to senior executives. In the Q&A portion, the CFO asks you a great question. You don't know the answer. You should, but you don't. So you either guess at the answer or make up the answer. Or you evade the question by changing topics and answering a different question.

**Solution:**

1. Don't fake it . . . ever.
2. Instead say, "That's a great question. I should know the answer to that, but I don't. I will find out and report back to everyone here."
3. Follow up with a great written answer to everyone who was at the meeting.

4. Be grateful for the opportunity to show both your humility and your competence.

**Critical Condition: " . . . but criticizes everyone." (see page 14)**
You dish out criticism in large portions. You consider it your personal mission to criticize everyone in the company, from senior management to the workers in the cafeteria. You are quick to point out every flaw in the CEO's presentation or eviscerate the latest advertising campaign. You criticize your colleagues and the quality of their work. You, the critic, like to sit safely and idly on the sidelines whispering things that undermine the people who are actually producing something.

**Solution:** You are being paid by your company to work and produce, not criticize. So get in the game and make something happen. Stop talking and start doing. Take some risk. Put yourself out there. Come out of the shadows and produce something that is worthy of notice. The people who get criticized the most are those who do the most. Be one of them.

**New—Defensive Player of the Year: " . . . but comes across as defensive when questioned."**
You can't take feedback or handle probing questions. When presenting or fielding management questions, you act as if you are being tried for war crimes at The Hague. You are defensive, evasive, or abrupt when asked questions. You seem to forget that everyone in the room is trying to get to the right answer for the benefit of the company. The collective knowledge of a room full of people is a powerful advantage that you

the presenter should use to improve your overall understanding of the risks and opportunities.

**Solution:** When asked a question try the following:

1. Clarify the question for everyone.
2. Acknowledge the validity of the question.
3. Answer it as best you can.
4. Solicit opinions and insights from others in the room.

Remember, being defensive is quite offensive when everyone is on the same team.

### New—Dying from Complications: " . . . but overcomplicates things."

You can make the simplest things ridiculously complicated. You seem to forget that the shortest distance between two points is a straight line. When faced with a problem or opportunity, you overthink the potential solutions. In an effort to be creative, you will devise an elaborate solution with too many dependencies, too much cost, and too much complexity.

**Solution:** When faced with a challenge, always start with the simplest solution and build out from there. Be that person in the room who speaks with clarity on the nature of the problem, its root cause, and the simplest solution for it. Time and money are saved with simplicity.

### Finish! First: " . . . but stretches herself too thin." (see page 56)

You try to do too much, and then you don't do anything very

well. They say that the road to hell is paved with good intentions. Saying yes to everyone who needs your assistance will put you on that road. You have trouble staying focused on the highest priorities when colleagues ask for help. Forgetting what your priorities are and taking on more than you can handle will result in shoddy performance and late delivery. Finish the most important task first.

    **Solution:** The best way to prevent this BUT from growing is having the courage to say no. Check in with your manager to review his or her top priorities. And don't be swayed by a needy colleague. Stay focused on the highest-priority task at hand and say "no" or at least "later" to all others.

### New—Frazzled: " . . . but becomes stressed out."

You can't handle the heat in the kitchen, and everyone knows it. You get totally consumed and stressed by leading a big project with a firm deadline. Frantic phones calls are made in the morning. A blizzard of emails are written at night. Your interactions with others are cold, terse, and racked with anxiety. You stress out the project team when you come blustering into the meeting. Everyone knows you are completely overwhelmed, and the team goes out of its way to avoid you so they can get the work done. In most cases, the project is delivered on time and on budget. However there is a cost for you, the frazzled person. The next project will be led by someone else.

    **Solution:** Remember the old saying "Never let them see you sweat." Be cool. Be calm. Let your colleagues do their thing. Trust but verify that the project is on track. Find outlets for your stress that work best for you. We find the best way to blow off steam is to go for a walk or hit the gym. Exercise lowers your blood pressure, releases endorphins into your system, and provides you a greater sense of well-being. When you feel the wave of tension and stress come over you, take it out on the elliptical machine, not on your colleagues.

**The Fred Sanford: ". . . . but passes off underperforming employees to other departments instead of dealing with them himself." (see page 124)**

You would rather pass along your junk than deal with it. You are a corporate Fred Sanford who gives good reviews to poorly performing employees in order to help them transfer to other departments. You lack the courage to manage or dismiss problem employees, so you facilitate their move to other departments.

**Solution:** Don't pawn off poor performers on your colleagues. Be a Truth Teller and confront the problem employees with their BUTs. It's your job to manage up their performance or manage them out the door.

**Gossip Girl and Boy: " . . . but loves to gossip." (see page 8)**

You love corporate gossip whether it's true or not. You take great pride in knowing and distributing the latest insider information. If someone wants to get information to the masses, they just share it with the Gossip Girl or Boy and say it's a secret. You are more effective getting the story out than the major news wires. You simply whisper in hallways and pull people aside at the water cooler, and word travels fast. Information is power, and you cannot wait to show off how powerful you are.

**Solution:** If you are a gossip, stop now! Don't tell other people's office secrets. If subordinates, peers, or managers share things in confidence, keep them to yourself. Nobody likes a gossip other than another gossip.

### New—Gutter Mouth: " . . . but talks like a truck driver."

People feel that you don't fit within the corporate culture. #@&%! is never the right thing to say in a corporate setting. When you are at work, be mindful of your language. Foul language cheapens you and often offends other people.

**Solution:** Keep the language clean at work. HBO can get away with it. You can't.

### The Hallway Hero: " . . . but then complains about and derides the decision afterward." (see page 115)

You often act like a two-faced traitor. Supporting a project or decision publicly in a meeting and then bad-mouthing it in front of coworkers is as low as it gets. If you have ever done this, you need to understand how destructive this behavior is to your company. An employee who subversively undermines the decisions and initiatives of his or her own company might as well be working for the competition. You are far more dangerous than any competitor, because you have access to information and can influence the views and attitudes of other people in the firm. The corrosive impact you can have on strategy and morale is frightening.

**Solution:** Perhaps your dissenting view is the correct one, but it's of no value if you do not share it. Don't be a coward. Share your opinion, and if the company still wants to proceed with the program, try a second time to dissuade them. If you are overruled again, you need to accept the decision and get on the bus. Your responsibility now is to do everything in your power to help the program be successful. That's what leaders and good employees do.

**Help Me Help You: " . . . but will not delegate." (see page 129)**

You want to do everything yourself and get all the credit. Every meeting, every assignment, and every task requires your engagement and attention. Why won't you delegate some of the important work? Why are you trying to do everything yourself? Perhaps you feel more secure in your job when you control all the tasks. Maybe you are distrustful of your direct reports and fear someone will screw it up and make you look bad. If you cannot delegate, you have limited upside potential because you will always be doing tasks that are below your rank. You need help, whether you know it or not.

**Solution:** In order to get more responsibility, you have to delegate tasks and responsibility to free yourself up for more important tasks. Delegation is something a good manager will do regularly. He or she is glad to provide their team members more responsibility and opportunities for growth. Get lower-level tasks off your plate and focus on higher-impact activities.

**High Maintenance: " . . . but is high maintenance." (see page 10)**

There always seems to be a lot more noise around a project when you are involved. While doing your job, you burn the time and waste the energy of everyone around you. An incessant array of meetings, phone calls, emails, and conflict resolution sessions inundate your manager and colleagues. These time-wasting activities sharply raise the cost of employing you and greatly reduce your value proposition to the firm. The problem with a high-maintenance person like you is that you are oblivious to the immeasurable cost of your never-ending needs.

**Solution:** If you have been given this feedback, ask yourself how much of your manager's and colleagues' time has been used up by issues that you have responsibility for. You need to think carefully before bringing your problems to others and burning up their time. Try to solve things on your own. Your manager has plenty of other things to do. If you do show up at your manager's door with a problem, make sure that you also have a solution. Companies are looking for people who deliver high productivity and require a low level of maintenance.

**New—The Houdini: " . . . but vanishes when things get ugly."**

You disappear when your team needs you. There is a major crisis in your company. Someone in your business unit made a mistake. The annual revenue target will not be met, and heads may roll. You choose to keep your normal meeting schedule, and you take your planned vacation. You want to distance yourself from the problem. Bad move.

**Solution:** You must be a first responder when major disruptions occur. You must be a highly visible and constant presence, reassuring your team that the crisis will pass. Come into the office early and go home late. Tell everyone it will work out even if you are not sure it will. Your people will remember who ran for cover and who ran in to help when the shooting started.

**Indecisiveness: " . . . but can't make a decision." (see page 75)**
You are seen as being incapable of bringing issues to a conclusion. Business leaders must take action. Yet you will not make a decision unless you have 100 percent of the information. You study report after report as the situation continues to deteriorate. This causes analysis paralysis and no actions are taken. Remember, you will never have 100 percent of the information, and there is no such thing as a perfect plan.

**Solution:** You have to aggressively engage a problem or a competitor in order to understand what you are up against. In business, action produces information, and information leads to adjustments. If your first decision does not get the results you want, then adjust. The more you do, the more you learn about the market and the competition, and the sooner you will reach your ultimate goal. Decisions are not scarce and they are not final. They can always be recalled, redone, or adjusted. Don't wait until you have all of the information before making a decision.

**Invisible Ink: " . . . but nobody seems to know you."**
**(see page 117)**

You are on nobody's radar screen for the next opportunity. You work very hard. You have a great skill set. You are unbelievably efficient and productive. The company gives you so much work that you never leave your cubicle. You work closely with your boss but you have very little contact with people outside your little world. If you keep your head down and keep doing what you are doing you believe you will be recognized and rewarded. Wrong!

**Solution:** You have to network. You want and need people to know who you are and what you do. You can get involved and meet people by volunteering for special projects, participating in corporate community outreach programs, or stepping up to organize the holiday party. Networking is not only incredibly valuable to shaping a career; it's also fun and rewarding. The most effective way to network is to befriend the people who are the best networkers. Every company has people who just seem to know more people and are known by more people. These people are easy to identify because they are positive and energetic and they know everybody. Become their friend, and you'll make many more friends.

**It Wasn't Me: " . . . but never admits a mistake." (see page 102)**

You want to be perfect, but you are not. You will not accept responsibility for anything that does not go as planned. No matter how clear your error is, you will create an elaborate self-reasoning loop that ends with the error being someone else's fault.

**Solution:** If you screw up, admit it and fix it. If a formal apology is beyond your reach, try this little expression to let the world know you are like the rest of us: "My bad." Those two simple words are unbelievably effective on the basketball court or in the office. "My bad" is an efficient proclamation of your humanity and your imperfection. Use it often.

### The Know-It-All: " . . . but comes across as a know-it-all." (see page 32)

You think you are the smartest person in the world. You take every opportunity to show the world how much you know about everything. You will cut off other speakers or finish their sentences for them. While you believe you are showing the world how smart you are, you're actually highlighting how insecure, selfish, and annoying you are. Over time, you will become increasingly isolated as your colleagues grow weary of trying to tell you something and repeatedly getting shut down.

**Solution:** Information is the most valuable asset in a company, and your obnoxious behavior will ensure you never receive any. Remember, you don't learn anything while you are talking. Stop trying to be the smartest person in the room. Once in a while, let the people around you be the smartest people in the room. You'll be surprised by how much you will learn.

### Lyin' Eyes: " . . . but has difficulty telling the straight truth." (see page 108)

Your honestly is questionable. You can have recollections of what was said or what was decided in a room that are dramatically different from everyone else. In some cases you forget what you said and committed to do. You spin the truth or the data in order to strengthen your position or move your agenda forward. There is a fine line between misremembering and lying, and if you walk it, you do so at great personal peril.

**Solution:** Anything less than 100 percent disclosure is a form of lying. As an employee, you have an obligation to provide your management and your colleagues all of the facts. Truth and transparency are the foundation of trust. Build and maintain that foundation.

**The Micromanager: " . . . but is a micromanager." (see page 122)**
You are an overbearing nag. You will give out an assignment with a future delivery date and then bother your reports for hourly updates and assurances on how they are doing. Your people never learn to think and fend for themselves, which impedes every aspect of their professional and personal development. Your team members will jump at the first job offer to get out from under your horrible management style. If you are a micromanager, know that talented people will not work for you.

**Solution:** Back off. Give your people some breathing room to develop their talents. Let them experiment. Allow them to make some mistakes so they can learn from them and grow stronger. Trust them to do a good job until they prove otherwise.

**Mr. Freeze: " . . . but freezes up in a crisis." (see page 31)**
You are paralyzed when the pressure is on. When you get

overwhelmed by multiple and simultaneous problems, you shut down. There are many things to be done, but, because there are so many, you freeze up and do none.

**Solution:** When faced with a multidimensional crisis, break tasks down into manageable pieces, and focus on the issues that you can influence and/or control. Don't let the larger, uncontrollable issues prevent you from acting decisively and moving forward on the achievable tasks. Think clearly and act decisively on the things you can positively impact.

### Mr. Softee: " . . . but is too soft with their people." (see page 128)

You are a wimp when it comes to difficult situations. You never make tough decisions. You don't confront bad employees. Problems linger. Conflict is avoided. You are a nice person, but you are losing the respect and confidence of your team.

**Solution:** Even if it's not your nature, many workplace situations require a hard-nosed toughness. Decisions must be made. Underperforming employees must improve or leave. Disruptive people need to be fired. Conflict must be welcomed, because it's the process that leads to the right answers. Toughen up! Or get out of the way and let someone else lead.

### New—Old Unreliable: " . . . but can't be relied upon."

You cannot be trusted with responsibility. You showed up late to the client meeting. The marketing letter you sent out had stale information and four typos. The project you led was two months late and 40 percent over budget, despite your earlier representations that it was on track.

**Solution:** Every day you are building your brand for integrity and delivery. You have to fulfill the commitments or word will travel fast that you need to be managed closely. Write down every commitment you make. Put the delivery date on your calendar. Make a project plan. Check and recheck the quality of your work. Deliver it on time and on budget.

**New—Panic! at the Disco: " . . . but panics at the first sign of difficulty."**

You go a little crazy at the first sign of trouble. The client is furious. You failed to deliver on time. They are canceling the account and threatening a lawsuit. You come out of your office screaming at your staff and declaring that this event might put you out of business. You call senior management and get them all riled up and buzzing. An hour later, you find out that the FedEx package has been sitting in the client's mail room since last Friday. In any company there are going to be unpleasant surprises that will threaten your business. Yes, bad things are going to happen, and you will have to deal with them. Competitors will steal a key client or take market share. A new regulation could put your business at risk or add significant costs to your enterprise. Angry clients will call you. What is most important about those setbacks is how you react to them. If you panic, your colleagues will panic. Not good.

**Solution:** No matter what the challenge, you have to confront the situation head-on and with a calm demeanor. Get the facts. Find out exactly what happened. Call the client yourself. You need to be calm, determined, and thoughtful in all of your actions and decision making during a crisis. People want cool leadership when the heat is intense. Don't disappoint them.

**New—Paranoia: " . . . but appears insecure."**
You think everyone is out to get you. Every slight is part of a grand plan to destroy you. You derail your own career by imagining that your colleagues are part of a covert conspiracy against you. When you are denied a promotion, it's because the boss hates you. When your proposal is passed over, it's because you are from the newly acquired unit, not the heritage firm. When your manager does not respond to your email, it's because he or she is trying to freeze you out of the project. You make stuff up to feed your insecurity and protect you from dealing with your shortcomings.

 **Solution:** The business world is not high school. Everyone is too damn busy to engage in cliques and mind games. If you did not get the promotion, it's because someone else was more qualified or a better fit. If your proposal got passed over, it was not good enough. If your boss did not respond to your email, perhaps there was a death in his or her family. Stop making stuff up! If things are not working out for you, look in the mirror before you blame the CIA.

**New—Politically Incorrect: " . . . but is so political."**
Your views are the same as those in power, whether they are right or wrong. You have a PhD in office politics. Everything you do is politically motivated. You know who is on the way up the corporate ladder and who is on the way down. You know

both the alliances and the warring tribes. You can separate the weak from the strong, and you align yourself accordingly. Your views and opinions are dictated solely by the audience in the room. You have no personal or professional views or judgments. You put your finger in the air to measure the political winds, and then you speak and act accordingly.

**Solution:** Steer clear of the office politics. Be your own person. Speak for yourself and not for others. If you completely align yourself with one leader over another in a politically charged environment, your career is now tied to that individual. Let your colleagues hear what you value and what you will fight for. Be yourself and not some shill for today's rising star that may burn out tomorrow. Your loyalty should be to the company, not to the people passing through it.

**Project Myopia: " . . . but does not take into account the views of others." (see page 58)**

You are excited about your project, and no one can stop you from doing it. You want to make it happen. Your colleagues see risk and challenges associated with your project. They want to share their views and have a thorough discussion. You plow ahead on the project and ignore or dismiss their concerns.

**Solution:** Slow down. What's your hurry? Take the blinders off. If your project can't withstand the scrutiny of your colleagues, perhaps it's not a good project. You should hear the other side. Then you should argue the other side and see if the benefits still outweigh the risks. Listen to and leverage the experiences of the people around you. The ability to argue vigorously both for and against any recommendation will help you make better decisions and highlight your thoughtful and balanced approach to decision making.

**Ready . . . Fire . . . Aim!: " . . . but acts before thinking."**
**(see page 76)**

You are a loose cannon. You send out the email before considering the consequences. You approve the larger budget before checking with your manager. You launch the new product campaign before getting buy-in from your independent sales reps. You take action before you have thought through all of the issues and risks associated with those actions. Sometimes it's impatience, and other times it's sloppiness that leads to premature action.

**Solution:** Take a little extra time to get your ducks in a row. Build some consensus before moving ahead. Remember that for every action, there is an equal and opposite reaction. Make sure you have thought through all of those potential reactions before taking aggressive action.

**New—Risky Business: " . . . but is too risk averse."**

You are weak and fearful. Business is all about taking and managing risk. You fear risk. You completely avoid uncertainty and ambiguity. You only see the downside of risk but never the upside. You are only half as good as people who see both.

**Solution:** Risk is everywhere. Do not fear it or avoid it. You need to study, quantify, embrace, and manage risk. Put logical probabilities on the possible outcomes and see if the expected value creation of taking risk outweighs the probability and size of a potential loss. Studying the numbers and imagining the scenarios will help you muster the courage to make a risky call. Risk is a prerequisite of reward.

### New—Scatter Brain: " . . . but can't focus."

You are all over the place. Someone has come to your office to tell you something. During the conversation you check your email, fire off a text, answer your phone, and change the topic two times. There is nothing more annoying when you are trying to communicate important information and the listener is distracted. This is not only rude but also creates an image of complete disinterest in what the other person is saying. How does that make them feel? How does that make them feel about you?

**Solution:** When people set up a meeting with you, give them your full attention. Don't check your smartphone, don't answer a call, and don't go off on tangential topics. They have something important to communicate to you, and you have an obligation to hear them out. Sit quietly, listen closely, and ask questions that clarify important points. Control your ADD so your colleagues can *add* some value and feel valued.

### New—Short Arms and Deep Pockets: " . . . but is cheap so we don't want to invite them."

You are a tightwad. You complain every time somebody at work asks you to contribute money. When you are approached to chip in for a wedding shower, baby shower, or a Girl Scout cookie purchase you get visibly annoyed. When you go out for drinks after work you point out the people who had a second round and tell them to pay more. Nobody likes a cheapskate. It's just a bad image to have.

**Solution:** It's important to be a good corporate citizen, and that often requires some separation of your money from you. Don't complain, and just pay your fair share. The stuff that costs you a few bucks is the glue that binds teams of people together. It will all come back to you in the future in some shape or form. Being a cheapskate is a "penny wise and pound foolish" career strategy.

### Sine/Cosine = Tangent: ". . . but goes off on tangents." (see page 26)

Your mind wanders and you waste everyone's time. Your team is discussing an important issue and you keep bringing up other issues or less important things. In today's business world, time is our most precious resource, and you do not use time wisely when you create distractions.

**Solution:** When speaking in meetings, stay on topic. Whatever the main issue or decision to be made is, be sure to stick to it. Tangential stories or issues waste time, dilute focus, and annoy everyone.

### The Talker: ". . . but never shuts up." (see page 3)

You, the incessant talker, like to hear yourself talk. Nobody else likes to hear you talk. You take ten minutes to communicate what could be said in one minute. You have no idea that people stopped listening to you nine minutes ago. People who talk too much can ruin a client meeting or suck the energy out of the room in the next management meeting. During one-on-one conversations the talker misses all the social signals that indicate the other person wants to end the conversation. If you speak a lot more than you listen, you likely have this problem.

**Solution:** If you are presenting in a meeting and your audience is not making eye contact, nodding in agreement, or asking questions, you probably lost them. Stop immediately and ask the audience questions about your presentation. Am I covering the issues you care about? Do you have any questions? Should I stop here? In a one-on-one conversation, if the person with whom you are speaking looks at their watch or phone or begins to type on their keyboard, they want to exit the conversation. If they say things such as, "Okay then," "Got it," "Well anyway," they want out, so let them go. Read the signals.

**Yes-Man: " . . . but is just a yes-man." (see page 110)**

You are a spineless flunky. You nod in agreement with everything your boss says. You think every idea your boss generates is a good one. To get people to do things you say, "The boss wants it that way," when that's not at all true.

**Solution:** Think for yourself. Have a view and express it. Your boss needs good counsel, not blind agreement. If your boss's ideas stink, have the courage to say so. If the boss doesn't want your input, go find a new boss.

# APPENDIX D

---

## RECOMMENDED READING

We hope that the concepts and insights of *Kiss Your BUT Good-Bye* have elevated your sense of awareness related to the aptitudes, personality traits, and behaviors you consistently put on display. We are confident that when you return to your workplace the BUTs of your colleagues will be bigger, bolder, and more obviously annoying than ever before. We will have accomplished our mission if our book has burrowed deep into your brain and you think of it often in the coming weeks and months. Good books stay with the reader long after the last page is turned. Below we have listed a few books that have stuck in our brains for the long term and they highlight some of the lessons we touched upon in *Kiss Your BUT Good-Bye*.

*Unbroken*, by Laura Hillenbrand (Random House, 2010).

When you learn what a former Olympic runner, Louis

Zamperini, endured serving his country in World War II and the resilience he displayed in the most horrendous of circumstances, you'll never again feel like you had a bad day at work.

*John Adams*, by David McCullough (Simon & Schuster, 2002). Our country's second president had a list of BUTs as long as the Declaration of Independence. John Adams was an impatient, arrogant know-it-all who was myopically focused on freedom from tyranny. If he didn't have all those BUTs we would all be speaking with British accents.

*Sh\*T My Dad Says*, by Justin Halpern (HarperCollins, 2010). The author's father appears to be an insensitive, foulmouthed, intimidating bully who verbally abuses his sons. As the book unfolds you realize the father is a loving "truth teller" preparing his sons for the adult world that awaits them.

*The Five Dysfunctions of a Team*, by Patrick Lencioni (Jossey-Bass, 2002). We would be remiss if we did not include one business title. This book highlights what happens when BUTs congregate and nobody communicates . . . nothing good.

*Undaunted Courage*, by Stephen Ambrose (Simon & Schuster, 1997). This is the story of Lewis and Clark's daring voyage to find the Northwest Passage. Business also involves journeys into uncharted territories, with roaring rapids and hostile competitors. Fight hard to keep the canoe afloat and just keep paddling.

*The Last Lecture*, by Randy Pausch (Hyperion, 2008). The author was a professor at Carnegie Mellon University who was diagnosed with terminal pancreatic cancer. He gave this lecture on "life lessons" just months before he died.

Here are a few gems lifted from his speech:

"If you're going to do anything that is pioneering you will get those arrows in the back, and you just have to put up with it." (BPUs are really good at archery.)

"Get a feedback loop and listen to it. Your feedback loop can be this dorky spreadsheet thing I did, or it can just be one great man who tells you what you need to hear. The hard part is the listening to it." (BUT-slaps hurt.)

"When you see yourself doing something badly and nobody's bothering to tell you anymore, that's a very bad place to be. Your critics are your ones telling you they still love you and care." (Honor thy Truth Teller.)

# ABOUT THE AUTHORS

JOE AZELBY IS a the managing director and CEO of the Global Real Assets Group of a large financial firm. He leads a team of more than four hundred investors that invests and manages $60 billion of real estate, infrastructure, and maritime investments across the United States, Europe, Asia, and Australia. Joe graduated from Harvard University with a degree in economics and later went on to earn an MBA in finance from New York University's Stern School of Business. While at Harvard, Joe was the captain of the football team before being drafted into the National Football League in 1984, where he played linebacker and special teams with the Buffalo Bills.

BOB AZELBY IS the vice president and general manager of the oncology business unit of a large West Coast biotechnology firm representing more than $5 billion in annual revenue. Prior to this role, Bob was the vice president of that company's U.S. Oncology Sales Team, which is made up of more than five hundred representatives. He received his bachelor's degree in economics and religious studies from the University of Virginia and his MBA from Harvard University.